BECOMING ONE

The Diversity Salad Bowl Open Mind

VOLUME 2

Becoming One: The Diversity Salad Bowl Open Mind—Volume 2
Copyright © 2024 by Rev. Dr. Albert R. Reddick

Published in the United States of America

Library of Congress Control Number: 2024921703
ISBN   Paperback: 979-8-89091-722-5
ISBN   eBook: 979-8-89091-723-2

All rights reserved. No part of this publication may be reproduced, stored in a retrieval system or transmitted in any way by any means, electronic, mechanical, photocopy, recording or otherwise without the prior permission of the author except as provided by USA copyright law.

The opinions expressed by the author are not necessarily those of ReadersMagnet, LLC.

ReadersMagnet, LLC
10620 Treena Street, Suite 230 | San Diego, California, 92131 USA
1.619. 354. 2643 | www.readersmagnet.com

Book design copyright © 2024 by ReadersMagnet, LLC. All rights reserved.

Cover design by Ericka Obando
Interior design by Don De Guzman

— Rev. Dr. Albert R. Reddick —

BECOMING ONE

The Diversity Salad Bowl Open Mind

VOLUME 2

CONTENTS

PREFACE vii

Chapter I: Becoming One Goals/Outcome 1
Chapter II: Presentation to the School Children: How Your Blind Spot Can Be Your Superpower 7
Chapter III: Forced to choose between Two False Choices which are Unreconciled 13
Chapter IV: The Historical Background of Racism in America Definition of Racism............................20
Chapter V: What is the Biblical and Theological Basis of Reconciliation? 36
Chapter VI: Introduction 58
Chapter VII: Embracing Diversity and Differences can unify our nation to become one. 67
Chapter VIII: What we all share and what we all have in Common 73
Chapter IX: Moral Courage is a rarer commodity than bravery in battle or great intelligence.....................75
Chapter X: America needs Reconciliation, Forgiveness, and Healing 87
Chapter XI: The Design of the Model 89

Summary..111
Notes 117

PREFACE

The Racial attitude in America appears to be reflected in its institutions (Legislative, Executive and Judicial) and leadership, and are inhibiting racial reconciliation with justice, and sidelining exploding Diversity. Racism as a contemporary phenomenon has historical pain and suffering, which must be overcome to empower the country, its citizens, and leaders for reconciliation with justice. The reality of institutional racism in the country toward the African American community needs new approaches and resolutions to develop structures for sustaining and nurturing a network of trained leaders and schools/colleges/University-based advocates skilled in cross-cultural communication. Racism is persistent and subtle. However, its negative effects upon its victims continue to be decisive. Those who are heirs of privilege due to social location may easily overlook the disabilities which accompany racism. On the other hand, those who are oppressed must constantly negotiate a means for survival with personal integrity.

The government/church should support and lead the struggle for overcoming racism in this nation. It is not easy to get the leadership of the country/ church to see the seriousness of the problem and the restructuring needed to meet the challenge so obvious to an African American observer and the victims of unlawful discriminatory practices.

Unlawful discriminatory practices occur because of race, ethnicity, color, religion, ancestry, age (40 and above), sex, national origin, non-job-related disability, known association with a disabled individual, possession of a diploma based on passing a general education development, or willingness or refusal to participate in abortion or sterilization.

The government/church can be a vehicle that points the way forward for liberation and reconciliation in a Christian context for secular/ministerial education for ministry and mission.

This manuscript is a model to empower government/Christian leaders to take on new roles as effective agents of reconciliation with justice and peacemakers in their communities. The model will provide training in reconciliation, mediation, proactive peacemaking, and cross-cultural communication, it tends further to focus on the transformation of an institution/nation.

The design seeks to create leaders in the area of government/personal, congregational, community, and global transformation, the country/church must itself go through a transformation and renewal process.

Further, this is a model by which the government/ church can experience transformation and renewal as it pertains to historical racism. In the end, the government/ church may become a more effective institution with learning to manage its diversity ideally. The model can be replicated throughout the country's institutions (government, academic institutions, and religious institutions. Further, to bring about an increased understanding of today's racial landscape, how it is changing, and the impact it will have on the country and our communities in the future. There are several features to this model.

The first component is the establishment of government/church support groups. Groups will be selected from government/church leadership. This group will journey with the author through this model.

They will:

To identify important/pivotal moments in the racial history of whites, African Americans, and Hispanics ex: The 1965 Acts signed into law in 1965 by Lyndon Johnson.

To examine the current political landscape and how it is impacting members of the White, African American, and Hispanic community.

To explore the feelings of community members toward such issues as integration, immigration, changing census numbers, economic imbalance among the races, et, informal but non-threatening sessions of dialogue. (A format and set of guidelines would be created in advance and followed by all participants.) Ex: We will not identify anyone that we refer to by name. We will, instead, use such words as "Someone I know…, An acquaintance of mine…, A certain politician…, etc.)

To plan a series of activities/events that are designed to increase interaction among community members and provide opportunities for conversation in a non-formal setting.

To work with members of the community to formulate a set of goals for the future that will lead to improved communication and increased racial harmony.

To establish a gathering place for meetings, activities, and events to be held.

Support government/ church leaders.

Be involved in the project (program)

Help evaluate their institution/ church's ministry needs.

Assist in guiding the government/ ministry leaders in designing the required Renewal Project that is to benefit the country/ church.

Provide counsel and support to the government/ ministry leader as needed.

Provide performance evaluation of the government/ ministry leader at intermittent stages and the conclusion of the program.

Title:
"Becoming One Vol II: The Diversity Salad Bowl Leads to Open Mind"

CHAPTER I

Becoming One
Goals/Outcome

This manuscript will help our communities succeed and flourish and get an opportunity to change the narrative and help the black community overcome the wounds inflicted from Past Racial injustice. Black Americans must learn to share with each other our goals and helping us be more vocal and shine as overcomers of Racism rather than non-patriotic.

Overview. At time in our nation when two powerful forces seen to be moving in opposite directions – increased racial diversity within our communities and a rising discontent from our citizens is to create a model of cooperation, community and commitment based on the principals described by Dr. Martin Luther King during his "I Have a Dream" speech in 1963.

After our preliminary discussions and assessment of the vacant school building in Siler City, we believe the 14,240 feet building on 2.5 acres of land has enough space to support out Becoming One Community Center, as well as provide adequate space to include Chatham trades, a food pantry, and office space for other non-profit organizations in our community. Such a dynamic collection of occupants will make this property a focal point for training, community building, economic development, and communications dedicated to Becoming One mission described above.

Our Guiding Principles. Our success at the Becoming One Center will be based on three pillars of unification across our diverse communities:

Reframe the dialogue between our citizens;
Emphasize he progress that has been made in race relations;
Develop programming the creates a sustainable cultural, economic, and social environment of respect and shared values for all our citizens.

Our Target Audience. While our nation longs for the kind of curriculum, programming, and dialogue we are offering at the Becoming One Center, we are targeting our work towards three primary audiences that we believe hold the most potential for our success: the youth, interracial couples, and the non-profit business community.

The youth are a natural fit for our work, since their values are still forming and their minds are hopefully open to a more divers nation. Additionally, young people are clearly more capable of carrying our message of unity and respect for a longer period of time than our adults. Interracial couples too are a powerful audience and example of Dr. King's dream, since they offer a unique perspective into breaking down the barriers he dreamed of when he described "little black boys and black girls will join hands with little white boys and white girls as sisters and brothers." These couples are a living example of the power of love; a love that is capable of breaking down all the barriers between people, regardless of race.

Finally, we believe that by including the non-profit business community in our work at eh Becoming One Enrichment Center, we can gain immediate credibility and fast-track the community building required for this kind of facility to be successful.

Our Facilities' Requirements. The opportunity to develop the Becoming One Center in Chatham County will help us share our dream of uniting, not only our community, but actively provide a living example of how all our citizens are

capable of mutual respect, civility, and cooperation. We chose Chatham County as the pilot city for out project, since we are confident that the fundamental values and predisposition towards unity already exist here. What remains is nurturing the untapped potential that Siler City and Chatham County possesses in Becoming One and then fostering it within our community, as well as sharing it outside our town.

The facilities requirements we seek at the school building are as follows:

A RECEPTION AREA where all our guests may be greeted and guided to the specific place that has attracted them to the Becoming One Center in the first place. (This establishes a formal management and monitoring of the building's occupants)

A TRAINING ROOM where our children can engage in lessons that nurture the kind of respectful, unifying approach we hope to instill in our all community children. (This established discipline and creates an environment that emphasizes the value of continued learning)

An indoors ACTVITIES AREA where our guests can release their abundant energies and channel their creativities towards positive, productive outcomes. (This space may include arts, science, cooking, or just hanging out by our children.)

An outdoors ACTIVITIES AREA where our children and parents can get outside to participate in larger projects that enhance their Becoming One Center experience. (Here we recommend gardening, sports, or kite-flying for the kids to soar!)

A COMMUNICATIONS CENTER where our children can establish relationships with children, adults, leaders, and benefactors from outside of Chatham County and communicate with others around the nation and the world. This will require some readily available technologies, like internet accessibility, audio-visual equipment, computer(s), and a projection screen for displaying content. We consider this communications center as the crown jewel of our Becoming One center, as it will provide the children (and community) a platform for discovering like-minded communities around the nation and world. Additionally, and most importantly, the Becoming One communications center in Chatham County will become the hub and model that will seed interest in our Becoming One program to other communities. By providing a successful example of our work at the Chatham County Becoming One Center, we believe that other cities and states will be attracted to our towns in order to, first, gain a better understanding of how we do it, and second, to launch their own Becoming One Centers in their own communities.

A COMMERCE CENTER where our community business partners can provide goods and services to the community. More importantly, our Becoming One Center business leaders can serve as role models and mentors to our Chatham County community.

Our Leadership. The Chatham County Becoming One Center will be a public-private partnership between The Becoming One Community Enrichment and Diversity Center, Inc. and the local, county and state governments. On the private side, a Board of Directors, led by Dr. Albert Redick and Dr. John G. Duesler, Jr., co-founders of TheDialogue.tv will guide the strategy and oversight of the project. Dr. Duesler's and Dr. Reddick's executive experience in business operations, community development, and charitable organizations is an ideal fit for this project. From the public side, we anticipate that our Chatham County Board of Directors will provide our primary guidance on this project, and that our county and state officials will be attracted to our work, as we witness its unifying affect, economic impact, and creative empowerment throughout the county.

Funding Model. Adopting the well-established elements of a public-private partnership. The Becoming One Enrichment Center will pursue funding from three primary sources of revenue.

Private Funding: These revenues will be derived from rents collected from our partnership non-profit organizations that share the space with us, individual charitable donations solicited during our fund-raising campaigns, and corporate support that we target by advocating our mission of unifying the Siler City ad Chatham County communities with our Becoming One programming and training.
Public funding: The donation of the building we are interested in will be a demonstrable first step in creating partnership between the Becoming One Enrichment Center and Chatham County. Since we anticipate locating a number of local non-profits into this building will provide a significant economic impact to the city and county, we are open to any reasonable sources of funding that the city and county may provide, whether in direct revenues or in tax incentives to reduce our overall expense.
Government and Institutional Grants: Since our mission is so timely and in-front of the American public at this time, we believe that the mission of our Becoming One Enrichment Center is a highly desirable target for grant underwriting. Our research suggests that there are a number of governmental and institutional funding sources currently available that would entertain grant proposals related to our work.

Our Challenge. The challenge that we face regarding secured funding sources for the Becoming One Enrichment Center is knowing that we have Chatham County's commitment to locate our operations in the building. This "chicken-and-eggs" scenario puts us in an awkward situation, actually having a location to conduct of activities. Therefore, our objective at this point is to obtain Chatham County's

Agreement in Principle for us to assume responsibility for the school building, so that we can:

Demonstrate a tangible commitment from the county that they too are committed to making the Becoming One Enrichment Center a tangible reality:

Demonstrate to the Chatham County citizens that the mission of strengthening its community relations and unifying its citizens is a priority:

Provide proof of physical location where the Becoming One Enrichment Center would operate:

Begin gaining community support throughout the Chatham County's non-profit community to join us in rallying all our energies towards enhanced community relations: and

Demonstrate to the state of North Carolina, as a whole, that Chatham County's Is proactive in anticipating the cultural, economic, and social needs of its citizens, and be regarded as a positive example of community development for the entire state.

Conclusion. The Chatham County Becoming One Center is a pilot project to fulfill the urgent need that our community and our nation has at developing a mutual respect and greater unity amongst our citizens, using the curriculum and guiding principles of TheDialogue.tv, the Becoming One Center will provide an example to the rest of North Carolina and to the nation that we are capable of achieving many of the dreams that Dr. Martin Luther King described so eloquently in this 1963 speech in Washington, DC. We look forward to carrying on that legacy of radical love, so that Siler City and Chatham County, like America, can reach its full potential as great community and as a nation.

CHAPTER II

Presentation to the School Children: How Your Blind Spot Can Be Your Superpower

Speech delivered to students at Silk Hope Middle School, Chatham County School System by Rev. Dr. Albert Reddick President/CEO Becoming One Enrichment Diversity Center Inc.

Good morning.

As we begin, please close your eyes, and look out into the world...your world...our world.

What do you see?

[entertain answers from the children for just a few minutes. They may need prompting, like, "Do you see your family? Do you see your home? Do you see fairness? Do you see suffering? Do you see hope? It is essential that you evoke at least one or two responses from the students before you continue.]

Now...before you open your eyes back up, look past now and look into the future...your future...our future. How is it different from what you see now? How is it the same?

What do you see in the future?

[Again, the hope here is that a few students will respond. If it begins to get chaotic and the students become energized, then you are well on your way to a successful dialogue.]

All those things are valid and true...because that is your vision. And that is your truth.

Here's the thing about what you see...now...and in the future. Your vision...that which YOU see...is blind to everything else that is out there in the world. What you see now...and in the future...can only come from what is in front of you, what YOUR experiences have been, and how YOU think about the world. And that is a very limited perspective, when you consider the billions of other people whose eyes see the world too. We only have our own eyes to see, our own minds to think.

But that is okay! It is really okay, because of the fact that we ALL have a blind spot when it comes to how we think, what we see, and why we believe in what we believe in. It is this blind spot that I would like to discuss with you today, since understanding your blind spot will help you accept your past, manage your present, and prepare you for the future...right now...a day from now...a week from now...a lifetime from now.

KNOWING that you have a blind spot...having such an awareness of your limited point of view...understanding that you do NOT have all the answers and that you do NOT know everything is NOT only essential but can indeed be your superpower as you move forward in your lives.

Yes...this may be confusing to you right now. How can NOT knowing, especially as we site here in school trying to learn as much as we can...how can NOT knowing and having a blind spot in our lives be a superpower?

BECOMING ONE

That is a great question, so let me address it here in three ways.

(humility/past) The moment that we realize we are "not all that" is the moment you come to a better understanding of what it means to be human. And I share this with your generation who value "influencers," social movements, and smart taglines that many rally behind. In most of these cases, our intentions are good, are pure, are real...but they still cannot escape the blind spot we all have in EVERYTHING we do, EVERYTHING we think, and EVERYTHING we believe.

Quite simply, we cannot do EVERYTHING; we cannot know EVERYTHING; we cannot understand EVERYTHING... and that is okay, because we are human! And to be human means to be limited, to make mistakes, to be imperfect... and here is where the superpower part comes in...once we understand that we have this blind spot, once we understand this tendency towards being imperfect, once we understand that we make mistakes, once we understand that we do not know everything ...we now have the superpower to forgive ourselves for our imperfections, our mistakes, our ignorance.

And while we, you and I, should always be striving to do better, admitting your own personal blind spot will allow you to accept where you come from, who you were, the mistakes you have made, and help you to continue to try and try again without giving up. That is TRUE FREEDOM. And that is a superpower indeed.

(awareness/present) By living your life, every day, knowing that you carry this blind spot with you everywhere you go, you now carry the superpower of thinking more carefully about what is in front of you, right now. By understanding what you see, what you hear, and what you feel is NOT a complete picture, you can proceed each day with greater care to make better decisions.

In today's world, there are plenty of shiny objects, plenty of people fighting for your attention, but most of these folks are indeed imposters...and being aware of your blind spot will help you resist the temptations to chase those shiny objects: that hollow promise of feeling better through chemicals, that false reward of cheating on your homework, that momentary ecstasy of a girlfriend or boyfriend.

Being aware of your blind spot in that moment will help you to ask important questions in that moment: What don't I know here? What is next if I do this thing? How will this decision affect my life moving forward? All these questions come from a self-awareness that admits one simply thing...I just do NOT know right now...but that rests in your superpower to resist such impulsive, destructive, and consequential decisions... UNTIL YOU DO KNOW! Or at least until you are willing to admit that it is OK to NOT do something...at least for now.

Being smart is knowing what you want, but wisdom is knowing what you do NOT want! So make wisdom your superpower through being aware of your blind spot.

(empathy/future) And perhaps the most powerful thing about admitting that you have a blind spot is knowing that other people have blind spots too! Such an understanding lays the groundwork for THE MOST EFFECTIVE SUPERPOWER you will have in your life...empathy; feeling the pain, joy, and confusion that others feel around you.

Why is this the most effective superpower? Think about it. What is it about your best friend that you value the most? What is it about your parents that frustrates you the most? My guess is that it ultimately has something to do with "They get you" or "They don't get you." In other words, your best friend feels the same way you do and your rivals do not!

This is how empathy creates a bridge between you and others. Understanding that others too have this blind spot helps us avoid judging others, rushing to conclusions, and, worst yet, ridiculing those that we are closest to. We are only afforded a partial glimpse into the world of the people around us, no matter who close we think we are to them. Their trials, their tribulations, and their turmoil are most often hidden from us because of shame and guilt. Upon simple reflection, we must remember that others too have their own blind spots, and this frees us from the weight of accusation, resentment, and our own validation at the expense of others.

As important, the patience and understanding that empathy brings with it results in a personal freedom that helps your light glow bright in the world and that is attractive to those around you. Avoiding the knee-jerk judgement of others misfortune and shortcomings brings us all closer to union with others and demonstrates a superpower that will stop people in their tracks, since you will break the momentum of backsliding and piling on that we see so prevalently now in our virtual and human discourse.

Feeling the joy, sorrow, anxiety, and satisfaction of those around you are only possible with the awareness that our blind spot is not unique to us. All our fellow humans have a limited gaze on the world, and our appreciation and acceptance of that results in an empathetic gift that some may find threatening, but that will ultimately help you demonstrate your superpower in a way that ripples throughout those around you.

Yes…this form of a superpower can be difficult to understand and appreciate…

How can NOT knowing be a superpower?

How can being blind be a superpower?

REV. DR. ALBERT R. REDDICK

How can admitting my shortcomings be a superpower?

The answer to all these questions is easy…because each one of these answers, just like admitting we all have a blind spot is based on THE MOST IMPORTANT characteristic each one of us chooses to possess…or not…HONESTY!

Not honesty as a weapon for blunt talk…but honesty as a tool for admitting that we make mistakes, for appreciating that life is not perfect, for motivating us to always do better, and, most of all, honesty as a way for us to offer our incredible talents in the service of others.

If you are honest, then you can serve.

If you serve, then you can lead.

If you lead, then you can make the world better.

And that is my message for you today…make the world better by being honest.

Thank you!

CHAPTER III

Forced to choose between Two False Choices which are Unreconciled

"Fear of something is the root of HATE for OTHERS and will eventually DESTROY the HATER" (George Washington Carver 1864-1943).

I may not agree with what you say, but I will defend to the death your right to say it" (Voltaire 1694-1778).

As I would not be a slave, so I would not be a master. This expresses my idea of democracy. Whatever differs from this to the extent of the differences, is no democracy" (Abraham Lincoln 1809-1865)

In today's world, we are forced to choose…
   –From Paper to Plastic at the grocery store
   –Boxers or Briefs
   –Blue Devils or Tar Heels

To more heavy-hitting contrasts, like…
   Black Lives Matters or Law Enforcement
   Church or State
   Democrat or Republican

The tragic flaw with these FALSE CHOICES is that there are only TWO OF THEM! That these choices are IRRECONCILABLE or that today's choices, as famed almost everywhere we go, capture the enormous complexity we face in this nation...culturally, economically, morally, politically.

Is that far-fetched to place great value on civil rights, while at the same time supporting the police? Is it realistic to hold forth that The Church maintains a monopoly on moral standing and the greater good, while our governments are devoid of any moral compass guiding our policies? If we are either a Democrat or Republican, are we then expected to blindly subscribe to the platforms and platitudes of our party, all-white firewalling off any ideas from the other?

Sadly, these false dichotomies are all too often accepted and more importantly, adopted and internalized as the guideposts for how our nation should conduct its affairs. But even more disturbing, these either/or scenarios are FORCING us to choose sides on issues that can only marginalize us, at best, but WILL POLARIZE our communities at worst, all while shredding the fabric of our society one painful tear after another.

Evils of racism have been addressed on many levels and from many angles. However, the subject of urgency (to overcome racism) is somewhat unique. Indeed, much of what is written on the broader subject can lead us to conclude that the pervasiveness of racism and its systemic nature renders any near-term solution unattainable. From this comes a complacency that will undermine a sense of urgency in the fight against this evil. Therefore, this topic is timely and important.

The Power of Forgiveness: Tool to Overcome Racism without Reparation & For African Americans to overcome Black on Black Crime/ Stop Targeting Police

Finding Peace

While struggle has always been an inescapable aspect of our lives, these days the struggles seem to be gaining momentum. They seem more difficult and more consequential.

What used to be relatively easy is no longer easy.
What used to be automatic now requires great effort.
What used to be unspoken is now out in the open.
Where there used to be restraint, we now find no hesitancy.
And people have no problem telling us how we should live, what we should do, and how much they matter.
Wow!
It is no wonder, then, how the world at large now, not only holds onto resentments, but shares their resentments out in the open for all to see…as if their "openness" is a badge of honor to be celebrated.
How often do we hear our people talk about, "Well I have a right to my emotions," or "I'm just being honest."
Such dialogue, while understandable on its surface, is a symptom of a deeper reality. One whereby each individual feels entitled to having their judgements, their opinions, and their point of view out in the open in order to gain some sort of self-importance. The casualty of this transformation is the move away from our collective efforts that support our culture, our community, and our planet.
We cannot blame these self-important folks for their behavior. As I stated, the struggles have become more profound and more pronounced.
Why?

Because our belief that we can do anything, we can say anything, we can achieve anything is misinformed. Indeed, our lives are finite. Our planet's resources are limited. Our abilities are incomplete.

We are the product of our experiences, which, by definition, means we have blind spots, biases, and behaviors that we cannot escape!

And Jesus recognized this on the cross. Remember what he said as he hung there in unimaginable suffering…" Forgive them Father for they know not what they do."

Do we live our lives with that same openness and acceptance and selflessness that puts us in our sisters' and brothers' shoes wondering why they are so angry or so depressed or so dependent upon drugs?

Do we suspend our own hurt feelings or drama to imagine and understand the plights of those around us; their limitations and their blind spots?

Can we bring ourselves to forgive those around us who have hurt us, who have threatened us, who have jumped ahead of us in line to grab the last of those finite resources available in the world?

Forgiveness is not easy. It may not even be natural. But is entirely necessary if we are to free ourselves from the bondage of resentment, of anger, and of retribution. These are heavy weights to carry in our lives and, more importantly, they are not Godlike!

Harboring these negative emotions keeps us from shining God's light on the world. Obsessing on how we've been wronged and on what we are going to do to "make it right" distracts us from our true calling and the limits our true potential. Focusing in on the suffering wrought by our torturers and those who metaphorically have nailed us to the cross, keeps us just hanging there with no chance of salvation.

So how we do we forgive? How can we change our ways and move towards reconciliation? What are the steps we need to better appreciate the blind spots, biases, and behaviors of others? Let's take a look at that.

First, and foremost, we need to pray for an open mind. Remaining in the straitjacket of our past experiences will only limit the good we can do in the world. Without an open mind, the world is firewalled off to the endless possibilities of peace that forgiveness can bring us.

With an open mind, we can receive the light, even if it is only as a small flicker to start, that can help us develop and move even closer to God. Having an open mind starts on the path to our next stop along the way to reconciliation…and open heart.

An open heart now moves us into the planning phase of forgiveness. If an open mind is our gateway to seeing the world in a new light, then an open heart allows us to sense the world around us with greater awareness, We can now begin letting go of our past constraints.

When we develop a greater sense of the open and vast world around us, without be threatened by it, we are free to forgive ourselves and better appreciate where our brothers and sisters are coming from. Clearly, Jesus had this open heart as He continued his teachings, even after the denials of Peter, the betrayal of Judas, and the condemnation of the crowds that lead to his execution.

While this is an extreme example, if we could move just a fraction closer towards this form of an open heart, then our journey towards forgiveness will be further enhanced and become more possible. An open heart is essential on our path to forgiveness, and we cannot take this lightly. Once achieved, though, an open heart will then lead us to the final, most difficult, stage of fostering forgiveness: an open will.

This open will, coming because of an open mind and an open heart, is the one that requires the most courage.

While we can instinctively "know" what needs to be done, as well as put a plan together that we believe will be effective, it is not until we act upon our knowledge that we can make any difference in the world today.

An open will is the last phase in our obligation to forgive. This powerful transformation, both individually and institutionally, will result in an attraction and a "letting come" whereby we can openly and respectfully share our concerns. Such a shared process is where the most powerful forgiveness and reconciliation comes from.

This new open will stance creates an ecosystem that, most importantly, moves us away from our own thoughts, and ego, and helps us discover new ideas and intentions. These new/shared thoughts can now be tested to see what works.

Perhaps the most revealing aspect of this open mind, open heart, open will three-step is that true forgiveness is NOT a state of being, but rather a process. Merely saying, "I forgive you," without working through a personal transformation is lip service, indeed, and will not lead to the healing that is necessary for real forgiveness.

However, if we are able to do the hard work of transforming ourselves through prayerfully gaining these three levels of openness, then it may just be possible that, we as a community, can further provide forgiveness for a scarred and sacred past. A past, that going to back to the very beginning of this sermon, has kept us in bondage with history, with our nation, and with ourselves.

The transition from personal forgiveness and collective forgiveness is a long journey however. And this journey is one that has been delayed repeatedly, as we continue to cry our individual tears of sorrow and suffering. We stay stuck in the injustices of the past, while time itself continues to flow on past us, leaving us as a people to bear the burdens of history despite the advancements we collectively contribute culturally and civically.

The weight we carry is heavy and it continues to hold us back. And if we cannot, as a people, find the capacity for reconciliation… for forgiveness…for true freedom, then we as a people will remain shackled with the chains of repression and oppression and dehumanization that marks our time here in America.

So I am here today to share with you our tears of repression and oppression and dehumanization. And to remind you that these same tears that drop from our eyes must come from all of us to form first a humble stream that seeks, someday, to connect to the vast ocean of material prosperity. But that stream cannot reach the ocean until each and every one of us cries the tears of forgiveness and reconciliation.

Our stream will stop short of freedom if we as a people do not cry together, pray together, and forgive together. For when each and every one of us, in our individual humbleness to God, finds it within us to forgive, then the waters of reconciliation will grow strong and wide. And these tear-filled waters will cleanse our hearts, will cleanse our souls, will cleanse our collective history, not for us to forget, but so that we may forgive.

And if we can open our hearts to the freeing power of forgiveness, that river will rise. It will rise with a power that lifts our people from the depths of our despair and carries us to that vast ocean.

If we can open our minds to the freeing power of forgiveness, that river will rise free of the bitterness and hatred that hold us down.

And if we can open ourselves up to the freeing power of God's Will and forgiveness, that river will rise with a majesty and a righteousness that will carry us to the promised land. A land where the power of our people are celebrated for the good and God-fearing people that we are. A land where our gifts are respected, and our ideas are shared. A land where we are free of the shackles of our past and buoyed by the hope for our collective future, once and for all.

So on this day of reflection, this day of soul-searching, this day of reconciliation, let us pray that we may all forgive, so that we may all be free.

Let us pray that we may all forgive, so that we may all be free.

CHAPTER IV

The Historical Background of Racism in America
Definition of Racism

Chapter three is concerned with the purpose of the model and the urgency to overcome racism in the church. In this chapter, we will put the racism experienced in the church in a national context. We live in a racist society. Unfortunately, the same racism one experiences as an African American in our country is to be found in a religious institution that prepares men and women to serve in the church of Jesus Christ.

Definition of Racism

What is Racism? It is an ideology that puts forth the belief that one group is superior to another. Racism puts in place an institution with the policy, power, and mechanics to enforce superiority.

"The policies and practices of racism dominate its economics, political, social, educational, criminal justice, and religious institutions.[1]"

Racism in the United States is based on the concept of whiteness, a powerful fiction enforced by power and violence.

1

Whiteness is a constantly shifting boundary separating those who are entitled to have certain privileges from those whose exploitation and vulnerability to violence is justified by their not being white.

Racism itself is a long-standing characteristic of many human societies. Justifying exploitation and violence against other peoples because they are "inferior" or different has a long history within Greek, Roman, and European Christian traditions. However, there is not a biblical foundation for racism based solely upon race. Further, The Ancient world was Devoid of Racism at the time of Pepe's Historic conquest of Egypt, the fact that his skin was Dark was irrelevant.

In more recent historical times in Western Europe, those with English heritage were perceived to be pure white. The Irish, Russians, and Spanish were considered darker races, sometimes black, and certainly non-white. The white category was extended to include northern and middle European people, but still even fifty years ago excluded eastern or southern European peoples, such as Italian, Poles, Russians, and Greeks.

In the last few decades, although there is still prejudice against peoples from these geographical backgrounds, they have become generally accepted as white in the United States.

The important distinction in the United States has always been binary---between those who counted as white and those who did not. Drawing on already established popular classifications, whiteness was delineated more clearly in the United States in the eighteenth century as slavery was introduced and distinguished from various forms of shorter-term servitude. The conflict between black and white men in contemporary American culture can be traced directly through history to the earliest days of chattel slavery. White males entering the New World were ill-adapted to making the difficult transition from Europe to the American frontier. As recent historical research indicates, the development of what was to become the United States was accomplished largely, if not primarily, by African slaves, men, women, and children alike.

Africans were the first to cultivate wheat on the continent; they showed their illiterate masters how to grow indigo, rice, and cotton; their extensive knowledge of herbs and roots provided colonists with medicines and preservatives for food supplies. It was the black man, wielding his sturdy axe, who cut down most of the virgin forests across the southern colonies. And in times of war, the white man reluctantly looked to his black slave to protect him and his property. As early as 1715, during the Yemassee Indian War, black troops led British regulars in a campaign to exterminate Indian tribes. From Christopher Attucks to the 180,000 blacks who fought in the Union Army during the Civil War, black people gave their lives to preserve the liberties of their white masters.

Social Darwinism –Race as a Category

Although a racial hierarchy was in place from the time of the earliest European settlers, racism was only defined scientifically as a biological/genetic characteristic about one hundred and fifty years ago with the publication of Darwin's Theory of Species Modification and Linnaeus System of Classification. These ideas were combined by others into a pseudo-scientific theory, eventually called Social Darwinism, which attempted to classify the human population into distinct categories or races and put them on an evolutionary scale with whites on top. The very category of race denoting primarily skin color was first employed as a means of classifying human bodies by Francois Bernier, a French physician, in 1684. The first authoritative racial division of humankind is found in the influential Natural System of the preeminent naturalist Carolus Linnaeus.

The original classification consisted of three categories Caucasoid, Mongoloid, and Negroid. These were not based on genetic differences, but on differences that European and European, Americans perceived to be important. They were, in fact, based on stereotypes of cultural differences and measures of physiological characteristics such as dark skin, large nose, nappy hair, and skull size.

There was a complex and dynamic interplay between the popular conception of race and the scientific categories, neither of which was grounded in physiological or biological reality, but both of which carried great emotional import to white people. These theories had devastating consequences to people of color, regardless of how they were being defined. Theories that claim to provide a scientific basis for white racism are peculiar, post-Enlightenment by-products of modern civilization.

Although a few scientists still try to prove the existence of races, most scientists have long ago abandoned the use of race as a valid category at all.

Human variability is so large and so widely dispersed that no racial grouping or distinction is useful or justified.

There are tremendous genetic differences or variations within racial groupings and huge overlap between them, making the race categories themselves useless.

Genetic differences among humans can be explained by the distribution of genetic variables and don't correspond with any useful category of race defined genetically, by skin color, or any other physical characteristic. That hasn't stopped many people from believing that distinct races exist and from trying to use scientific language to buttress their arguments. There is, likewise, no scientific (e.g., biological or genetic) basis to the concept of whiteness. There is nothing scientifically distinctive about it except skin color, and that is highly variable. All common wisdom notwithstanding, the skin color of a person tells you nothing about their culture, country of origin, character, or personal habits. Many scenes have depicted this procession, but never have they shown the truth. The man chosen by the Romans to help Jesus carry his cross was a black Jew, Simon of Cyrene. "Now as they came out, they found a man of Cyrene, Simon by name, Him they compelled a certain man, Simon a Cyrenius, the father of Alexander and Rufus, as he was coming out of the country and passing by, to bear his cross." (Mark 15:21) "Now as they led him away, they laid hold of a certain man. Simon a Cyrenius, who was coming from the country, and on him they laid the cross that he might bear it after Jesus." (Luke 23:26) The scripture did not record any incident of protest or color distinction or racism because of Simon's blackness. However, as he carried Jesus' cross a great multitude of the people followed him, including women who also mourned and lamented him. (Luke 23:27)

The question then arises if the early people in the Bible were blacks and Afro-Asiatic, why isn't the color of their skin emphasized to a greater extent? The answer is simple. The writers of the Bible, together with the Greeks and the Romans, had a notion of color prejudice. In our society today, the idea of a world before racial discrimination is startling. The wonderful result of the lack of racial prejudice in the Bible is that the greatness of African peoples and their warrior (Genesis 8), is a prime example of the African character.

"Since the Bible is multi-racial and multi-cultural, the question has been raised, what color was Jesus? We can now return to the question of the race of Jesus of Nazareth[2]." His mother, Mary, was Afro-Asiatic and probably looked like a typical Yemenite, Trinidadian, or African American of today. Consider a few inescapable factors that challenge the traditional perception of the Madonna and Child. In Matthew 2:15 and Hosea 11:1 we find the words, "out of Egypt I have called my son. "The passage is part of the notorious flight into Egypt, which describes Mary and Joseph's attempt to hide the one that King Herod feared would displace him. Imagine the divine family as Europeans hiding in Africa. This is quite doubtful. Egypt has always been part of Africa, despite centuries of European scholarship which has diligently sought to portray Egypt as an extension of Southern Europe.

Hundreds of shrines of Black Madonna have existed in many parts of North Africa, Europe, and Russia. These are not weather-beaten misrepresentations of some original white Madonna but uncanny reminders of the original people who inhabited ancient Palestine at the time of Jesus of Nazareth and earlier. The Sweet little Jesus Boy of the Negro spiritual was, in fact, quite black.

Mary, Joseph, and Jesus were neither Greek nor Roman. With the marvelous oils and Watercolors of the painter's brush, the world gradually witnessed the rebirth of Jesus, as medieval and Renaissance artists made him suitable for the portrayal of Christianity as a European religion. Thus, there developed a brand-new manager scene, with the infant Jesus and his parents re-imaged. Ancient darker, and more African, icons were discarded or destroyed.

2

Many in the 1990s who think of a black Jesus as an oddity or scandalous distortion of historical facts insists that Jesus was Semitic, or Middle Eastern. However, to call Jesus Semitic does not take us very far, because this nineteenth-century term refers not to a racial type, but a family of languages including both Hebrew and Ethiopian. At about the same time that the European academy coined the term Semitic, it also created the geographical designation called the Middle East—all to avoid talking about Africa! Thus, academic racism sought to de-Africanize both the sacred story of the Bible and Western civilization.

Forms of Racism

What was the first instance of racism in the American Church? After purchasing his freedom Richard Allen returned to Philadelphia and took odd jobs: cutting cordwood, laboring in brickyards, and driving a salt wagon during the American Revolution. As Allen traveled he made acquaintances with some of the great evangelists in the Methodist Church and was permitted to preach as an evangelist although he had not been ordained, because, as Howard Gregg states in his History of the A. M. E, Zion Church, from the very beginning of Methodism in America Negroes were permitted into the various societies. Richard Allen was able not only to attend worship services but to speak. He was present at the Christmas Conference, which was the founding convention of the Methodist Church in America, which met in Baltimore on December 25, 1784. At the conference, Francis Asbury was elected a deacon, an elder, and a bishop within three days. He subsequently invited Allen to join him on a preaching mission to the South. However, Allen found the living conditions offered him to be unacceptable. Rather than sleeping in the carriage while Asbury would be allowed to enter hospitality inns, Allen decided to stay in Philadelphia. He joined the OLD St. George Methodist Church because in his heart he believed that the Methodists were more sensitive to the concerns of the slaves and freedmen than any other denomination. It was at Old St. George that he continued to nurture the relationship that had started when he worshipped earlier on the plantation, it was also in St George, when Allen encountered blatant racism, that the seeds of African Methodism were planted.

The tragic events that led to the walkout at Old St George Methodist Church started when blacks were separated from whites in worship, initially blacks were required to sit in the balcony. However, as they grew in number some were permitted to stand around the wall on the lower level even if seats available. The atmosphere was poison, and a resolution was initiated to have Allen preach to the black worshippers at 5 a.m. However, the hostility created by the attitudes of the white who expressed total dissatisfaction with blacks worshipping with them grew to intolerable proportions. Although Allen and his followers had a designated time for their worship, they also participated in regular worship. The hostility became exacerbated to the point of total indignation when on a certain Sunday they were physically removed from the altar while on their knees in prayer and ordered to leave the church. Richard Allen gives his testimony of the events of that day as they are recorded by Doyle, Greg, Wadley, and other authors.

The walkout by Allen, Jones, and others from St. George's was viewed by many as an act that they should not have taken. Some blacks and most of the leaders of the Methodist Church felt that this act was unnecessary. In some ways, the striking of this blow for freedom represented to the white leadership of the Methodist Church an attack that revealed the difference between their preaching and actual practice which they were not comfortable in having exposed.

Allen's movement was brought about by the inability of the Methodist Church to reconcile the preaching and teaching of its ministers to the reality of the conditions under which blacks were living.

Racism is any attitude, action, or institutional structure that subordinates a person or group because of their color. Institutional racism is such subordination occurring through the action or practice of some stable social arrangement, such as a school, business, or church.

Racism takes many different forms, but probably the most prevalent is institutional racism that affects agencies and organizations. Institutional racism occurs in the Christian church when believers operate out of ignorance, tradition, and the status quo, accepting the disparity between the races without questioning why. Institutional racism is often motivated by fear. Fear of the unknown, fear of people different from ourselves, fear of being inconvenienced, fear of losing our budget if we support this black program, fear that the quality of life is going to go downhill-all kinds of fear that motivate whites to respond in a self-preserving way. It seems strange that such fears would motivate the church that teaches and trains men and women to spread the gospel. What strange Christianity was in the Church? Racism always involves power. A very simple formula for racism is Power plus Prejudices equals Racism. Racism is different from racial prejudice, hatred, or discrimination. Racism involves having the power to carry out systematic discriminatory practices through the church in America.

What Is Overt Racism?

Overt racism is open and not secret. Before the Civil War, most African Americans were shackled with claims and confined to plantations. The American government maintained their lifestyle as slaves(chattel-property) and its criminal justice system, police force, and military might prevent their effective rebellion and escape to freedom.

During the American Revolution, over two thousand black slaves volunteered to join the beleaguered continental army of George Washington, a slaveholder. More than a generation later, two thousand black slaves from New York joined the segregated State Militia units during the war of 1812, and blacks fought bravely under Andrew Jackson at the battle of New Orleans. From Crispus Attucks to the 180,000 blacks who fought in the Union Army during the Civil War, black men gave their lives to preserve the liberties of their white masters. Yet blacks had no liberties, no freedom.

There were lynching and castration, Jim Crow, KKK, and up to the Brown versus Board of Education of Topeka et. Al. (1954). The separate and unequal doctrine was argued on December 9, 1952-reargued December 1953, and decided May 17, 1954. Segregation of white and Negro children the equal protection of the laws guaranteed by the fourteenth Amendment. Even though the physical facilities and others were available, white and Negro schools may be unequal. I believe this court decision started the shift from overt racism (open intentional and individual) to subtle and institutional racism. Additionally, the author thinks of school choice (scholarship)Title II. The Low-Income Educational Opportunity Act of 1966 is a revisit to the Brown versus Board of Education Topeka, Kansas, case.

The author believes it should not be necessary for a black person to be a super person to be accepted as a person. Most whites, most of whom are average, have a right to the good life in the country; why cannot the ordinary person whose face is black be self-affirming and likewise enjoy the promise of America?

In my view, all Americans should be self-affirming. Racism is serious and destructive. Former president Bill Clinton refers to it as the racial divide. It is more than a racial divide; it is a ticking implosion waiting to detonate. But I believe reconciliation with justice can aid in bringing about the radical measures needed to eradicate it. However, reconciliation without justice is what Dietrich Bonhoeffer calls "cheap grace."

The writer further believes not only individual Christians but the church as an institution is condemned by racism. It is my view that the institution that prepares leaders for the church is condemned by racism.

The reality of institutional racism in the church toward the African American community needs new approaches and resolutions to develop structures for sustaining and nurturing a network of trained church-based mediators skilled in cross-cultural communication. Therefore, the church must be open to seek a deeper walk with God, which will strengthen it to risk the new mission challenges that the world of today and tomorrow present. The racial divide in America, racism, and reconciliation with justice challenges today.

He believes concerned white Christians engaged in charity work in black communities could render a more effective service through the humanizing and redirection of white power.

What is Subtle Racism?

It is very shrewd, keen, clever, and hardly noticeable. Generally, great planning and collaboration (joint labor) are required to put it in place. Subtle racism is an ideology that both puts forth the supposition that one group is inherently superior to another and puts in place the institutional mechanisms that advance and support that supposition. Ideology and institutionalized policies that will enforce and secure these propositions compose subtle racism.

Racism is not just the sum of all the individual acts in which white people discriminate, harass, stereotype, or otherwise mistreat people of color. The accumulated effects of centuries of white racism have given it an institutional nature that is more entrenched than racial prejudice. It is barely touched by changes in individual white consciousness. Therefore, it is difficult to see or know how to challenge institutional racism, since we are so used to focusing on individual actions and attitudes.

The results of these patterns are that faculty of color earn approximately 75% of what faculty with comparable qualifications earn. A faculty member of color, working in the same department, who was equally qualified, the same age, and with the same years of experience as her white colleague could be making $10,000-$15,000 less a year and have considerably less job security, tenure, and other benefits. This could be true without a single overt act of discrimination in the pastorate. Further, pastors of color in the United Methodist Church earn approximately 45% of what white pastors with comparable qualifications earn. This situation is brought about by what is known as subtle racism.

In a recent case in Media, Delaware County, Pennsylvania, a white apartment complex owners' subtle practice of racism was exposed. White apartment owners listed their vacant apartments without disclosing the address. Instead, they listed phone numbers to call with automatic answering machines. The message asked callers to leave a phone number and complete name and address. The owners would then determine the person's race, and if African American they would not return the call. Owners would listen to the voice on answering services, and if they suspected that the inquirer was Africa-American, they would not return the call. Owners would determine from the address and telephone number where the caller lived, and if the area were highly populated with African Americans, owners would not return calls. This is subtle racism and a direct violation of the Fair Housing Laws against discrimination in housing.

We have discussed and considered some of the causes of the race problem. It would seem evident, then, that the removal of the conditions which give rise to these causes would suggest itself as the most obvious approach to the solution to the problem.

We saw that race" as it is generally applied to humans, is scientific without justification and that as commonly used the term corresponds to nothing. We saw that the word is predominantly an emotionally loaded one, and we were able to trace something of its rise and development in what has invariably been background or matrix of strong feeling and prejudiced thought. Human beings may pretend that they are ruled by reason when they are, in fact, creatures of emotions.

It appears that reason and intellect play a minor role in human lives when confronting the race issue, and what part they do play is often confused and fragmented.

Let us be wise and frankly face the fact that most people are emotional creatures who use their minds mostly to support their prejudices. Prejudice is a passion with a logic all its own. There is little use attempting to correct this logic by demonstrating its falsity, for it is not the logic that is the cause of the false logic. Hence, we would be more effectively employed in trying to understand the sources of this prejudice than in correcting the insecure logicians.

Most individuals wish to know the kind of things that will support them in the culture, whatever contributes to that end is reality. People live by the values they learn from their culture. If we preach equality but practice discrimination equality will not be learned. What is done, not what is said, is the reality in which most people believe. A culture lives what it believes…., that is, it acts out what it believes in; it does not live by what it aspires to be. Men will fight to the death for what they believe, but not for the ideals in which they have no faith. America is racist because it acts out what it believes. Its laws, its institutions, its culture live what it believes.

Any culture or part of a culture that finds it necessary to create and maintain hostilities between different groups of people instead of encouraging their social development by mutual exchange and cooperation of interests to the advantage of all is sick, for the great principle of biological as well as of social development is cooperation, not antagonism. The former president of this nation has acknowledged a great racial divide, and the ongoing racial violence throughout this nation daily supports the conclusion that there is a sickness in the land.

Without reconciliation with justice, of which Genesis 33:4-11 is an example, no one can be free until all people are free. Race prejudice arises from the failure to make use of human potentialities, particularly the powers to relate to one another and to establish human ties. Those who exploit their society for their interest, whether they are aware of it or not, are working against the interests of their society. They produce imbalances, top-heaviness, and dissipative rather than cooperative conditions.

Definition of White Privilege

Who is to blame for this sorry condition? Surely not the ordinary person! When one accepts Christ in a racist church and goes out into the world and attempts to behave approximately like a Christian the person soon discovers that being persistent in the attempt is likely to lead to suffering the fate of Christ. To survive, a person finds it necessary to adapt to the conditions of life as they are. In doing so people fail themselves and their society.

Let us ask ourselves, therefore, to what it is that we adapt ourselves? Without enumerating the unhappy catalog, we may answer at once: to conditions as we find them. We accept and adapt ourselves to evil as if it were good. Is this the reflection of a failure of nerve, of courage? I do not think so. On the other hand, I believe that most people accept the world for what it is, believing that it is so ordered by some immutable powers that things are as they are because that is the way they are, and little, if anything, can be done to change them.

"You can't change human nature," is the common expression of this viewpoint.

If what I have said is true, then our only hope lies in the education of the right sort (cross-cultural/multi-ethnic). If we can succeed in reorganizing our system of education from top to bottom, making our principal purpose the cultivation of human beings living in one great cooperative enterprise with other human beings, we shall have gone a long way toward achieving a new society free of the racial divide. Children learn early that race prejudice, unlike other antisocial behavior, is socially sanctioned and has the approval of respectable people.

McIntosh acknowledged she was taught about racism as something that puts others at a disadvantage but had been taught not to see one of its corollary aspects, white privilege, which puts whites at an advantage.

This white privilege leads to unconscious oppressiveness toward African Americans. McIntosh, through close reflection, began to count how she enjoyed unearned skin privilege. In unpacking this invisible knapsack of white privilege, McIntosh listed conditions of daily experience that attach somewhat more to skin-color privilege than to class, religion, ethnic status, or geographic location. The following white privileges were observed:

I can, if I wish, arrange to be in the company of people of my race most of the time.
I can avoid spending time with people whom I am trained to mistrust and who have learned to mistrust and who have learned to mistrust my kind or me.
If I should need to move, I can be pretty sure of renting or purchasing housing in an area which I can afford and in which I would want to live.
I can be pretty sure that my neighbors in such a location will be neutral or pleasant to me.

I can go shopping alone most of the time, well assured that I will not be followed or harassed.

I can turn on the television or open to the front page of the paper and see people of my race widely represented.

When I am told about our national heritage or about "civilization," I am shown that people of my color made it what it is.

I can be sure that my children will be given curricular materials that testify to the existence of their race.

If I want to, I can be pretty sure of finding a publisher for this piece on white privilege.

I can be pretty sure of having my voice heard in a group in which I am the only member of my race.

McIntosh believes that we are taught to think that sexism is carried on only through individual acts of discrimination, meanness, or cruelty toward women, gays, and lesbians, rather than in invisible systems conferring unsought dominance on certain groups. Systemic racism has implanted in the minds of the general society that white skin in the United States opens many doors for white whether we approve of the way dominance has been conferred. Individuals' acts can palliate but cannot end racism. Social systems need to be redesigned. However, we need first to acknowledge their colossal unseen dimensions. White America needs to take ownership of the existence of white privilege. McIntosh concludes that most talk by whites about equal opportunity is about equal opportunity to try to get into a position of dominance while denying that systems of white dominance exist.

Lord, some people have curled up and died in a corner for no reason other than they lost hope When there is no hope, there is no life. Without hope we give up; we lose our will to fight, to trust, and to live. There are too many people in the world today who have begun to lose hope: those who hunger for life's basic needs but see no relief; those who see too many problems and cannot find a solution; those who have no self-esteem due to slavery, racism sexism, and white privilege.

We are living in one of the most frightening moments in the history of this nation. Democracies are quite rare and usually short-lived in human adventure. The precious notion of ordinary people living lives of decency and dignity—owing to their life chances—is difficult to sustain over space and time. And every historic effort to forge a democratic project has been determined by two fundamental realities; poverty and paranoia. The persistence of poverty generates levels of despair that deepen social conflict; the escalation of paranoia produces levels of distrust that reinforce cultural division. Race is the most explosive issue in American life precisely because it forces us to confront the tragic facts of slavery, segregation, Jim Crow, lynching, the civil rights movement, integration of American institutions, the separate-but-equal doctrine, affirmative action, multi-ethnic growth, and ongoing practice of racism by the church. In short, a candid examination of the racial divide takes us to the core of the crisis of American democracy. And the degree to which race matters in the plight and predicament of fellow citizens is a crucial measure of whether we can keep alive the best of this democratic experiment we call America. Since democracies, as the great Reinhold Niebuhr noted, approximate solutions to insoluble problems, I envision neither a social utopia nor a political paradise.

In these downbeat times, we need as much hope and courage as we do research and analysis; we must accent the best of each other even as we point out the vicious effects of our racial divide and the pernicious consequences it has had upon African-Americans. We simply cannot enter the twenty-first century at each other's throats, even as we acknowledge the weighty forces of racism, multi-ethnic diversity, and economic inequality. We are at a crucial crossroads in the history of this nation and the history of the church. We have two choices: either hang together by combating these forces that divide and degrade us, or we hang separately.

The church is currently updating its history book, and it should embrace the Pennsylvania Human Relations Act (Act of October 27, 1955, P.L. 744, as amended).

It should be inclusive of its historical/contemporary practice of racism and its commitment to reverse its behavior.

The issue of race is a fact of life, a major problem in America. For many people race is not simply an issue to be discussed in a remote, abstract manner, but is a burning, turbulent, harmful, hurtful question that impedes impinges upon, and controls their daily existence. For these people, the issue of race is a priority, since it controls their present and determines their future. No wonder a discussion of the race draws such a passionate response that many who have not experienced racism often find it difficult to comprehend.

But whether we have experienced racism or not, the issue of race is one we cannot ignore, no matter where we are on the variegated spectrum of humanity.

Since each of us occupies a spot in this spectrum, the issue of race can never be ignored. The church cannot escape the necessity of dealing with the issue of racism. The power divider separating white and black Americans is reflected in the church.

One who experiences race as an advantage will develop a perspective different from another who experiences race as a disadvantage, and a great chasm yawns between the two.

The church culture is racist. This project is not to antagonize, but to bring about healing for the land and justice for the oppressed. The church stands at the threshold of moving this nation toward reconciliation with justice between African Americans and the rest of the population.

The church must end its racist practices and ongoing harm to its African American citizens who have not yet received the opportunity to live out the American Dream. It will be a costly journey for the church to reconcile with the African American community. However, on the other hand, failure might shorten its existence.

CHAPTER V

What is the Biblical and Theological Basis of Reconciliation?

Biblical Warrants

In this chapter, we will explore the biblical and theological basis of reconciliation and its challenge to the church. A biblical mandate calls Christians to a ministry of reconciliation.

(I Corinthians 5:19) Jesus is proclaimed Prince of Peace, and a special blessing is invoked for peacemakers identified as the children of God. (Matthew 5:9) Christians hold an image of God as reconciler, as God in Jesus Christ reconciles the world to Himself. (II Corinthians 5:18) Therefore, believers, who have a special obligation to be ambassadors of Christ, are called to be peacemakers and agents of reconciliation with justice. Community violence and conflict are at odds with the Christian vision of God's reign, which provides that the children of God, especially children, widows, and sojourners, will be protected by God's love and sustained by their hope in God's presence, now and for eternity. At the core of Christian theology is the understanding that all people are empowered by the Holy Spirit to be agents of reconciliation with justice, inspired by faith and guided by scripture.

The time and the right man met. Only an exceptional mind, a rare spirit, and an abiding faith could bring about reconciliation with justice.

Millions of subjugated African Americans lived under the rule of a foreign race. They were always discontented and frequently rebellious. Economic and political problems became so severe that only utilizing vigorous black codes, fugitive-slave laws, lynching, mass murders ongoing by the KKK, and dehumanizing practices daily could white supremacy be maintained. The white-dominated male-controlled society raped African American women and girls.

They perpetrated cruelty on African American slaves daily and deprived them of the fundamental grounds for human existence. All this barbaric behavior by dominating white males points to the dark side of white America's character.

The act of reconciliation was meant to break down the walls in both temple religion and societal oppression White-dominated, male-controlled America has wrought great oppression upon African Americans. I feel the hurt, suffering, pain, and agony. At the same time, I hear the words of Mohandas K. Gandhi, African Americans have been truthful about the horrors and oppression perpetrated by white America. African Americans love this nation despite its dehumanizing treatment and have been responsible for its development and prosperity.

There is dishonor in being slave owners. When there is dishonor there is also a lack of courage and integrity.

America, dominated by whites, owned slaves and lacks the courage and integrity to take ownership of its barbaric deeds. White America lacks honor. This lack of honor, courage, and integrity is a barrier in initiating reconciliation with justice. However, African Americans (the oppressed people) who survive the institution of slavery and its ongoing racism must rise with courage and save this nation from its racial divide. The future belongs to African Americans. Truth and love accrue only to the humble.

This gospel of reconciliation with justice reached out to the powerless in society by transforming the lives of Samaritans, beggars, and others marginalized by society. The message of reconciliation with justice also reached out to the powerful: an Ethiopian treasury official was baptized: Roman military officers were filled with the

Holy Spirit; Roman jailers got saved, and the Apostle Paul was on his way to Rome to witness to Caesar himself.

Theological Perspectives What is Repentance?

The New Testament refers to three basic terms to talk about repentance. Metanoia translated means repentance. This Greek word means to change one's mind. Jesus' call to Metanoia demanded an unconditional turning to God.

It is believed to involve the whole walk of the person.

Epistrophe means to turn around. The Hebrew word for the turnaround is the shrub. Shrub appears more than 1050 times in the Old Testament.

Theologically, shrub refers to Israel---turning from sinful rebellion against Yahweh to total submission to God's will. This is expressed in the covenants.

Metametomai means to change one's mind or regret something.

These three Greek words and one Hebrew word have a common reality to which they point. They refer to the process of radical transformation of thoughts and actions initiated by divine grace. This happens when a person is drawn to faith in Jesus and submits to him without condition. Further, repentance includes the centrality of a judgment of grace on us and others.

Christians believe that the Holy Spirit enables this diachronic and synchronic representation of the universal significance of Christ's lives and situations. Hannah Arendt ascribes to Jesus the discovery of the social role of forgiveness. But this was surely already developed in Judaism, as in the book of Jonah, which Jesus himself cites about the repentance of entire cities. (Matthew 12:41).

Repentance is regret for past sins and must evidence a radical transformation of our relationship with God and neighbor. The Gospel of Mark links repentance to Jesus' whole message. "The time has come, "he said." The Kingdom of God is at hand: Repent and believe the good news." (Mark 1:15) Jesus commands his disciples to preach repentance and forgiveness of sins in his name. (Luke 24:47)

Forgiveness without repentance or repentance without forgiveness, the Spirit is the one who enables human transformation. By making Christ universally significant, the judgment of grace, and inducing our repentance as a component of God's forgiveness, Spirit guides us.

Forgiveness without the evidence of repentance can produce a cheap reconciliation. Theology is based on the importance of forgiving and repairing wrong.

Jesus was physically nailed to a cross as a concrete demonstration (demonstrative evidence) that we are forgiven of our sins and that our relationship with God, which had been severed by sin, has been restored. The cross enables us to trust that our relationship with God has been reconciled.

The cross portrays forgiveness and reparation as two important aspects of reconciliation. Costly reconciliation calls us not only to forgive but to repair wrongs committed, whether we were the offending party.

What is Justice?

Justice is an attribute of God and Jesus. In the New, Testament Jesus represents the justice of God. The New Testament contains a rich variety of terms relating to justice. These include freedom (Eleuthera), love (agape), mercy (eleos), equality (isotes), integrity (apothecia), commandment (entole), and law (nomos). Regardless of variations in New Testament attitudes about justice, the law of love, as derived from a precept in Old Testament social legislation, is central. "You shall love your neighbor as yourself" (Leviticus 19:18), while originally referring to other Jews, takes on wider implications ins the New Testament, where neighbor means another human being, irrespective of the person's race or class. (Matthew 5:4; Luke 10:29; Romans 13:9, Galatians 5:14, James 2:8) This passage correlates the love of neighbor (now including Gentiles) with a mandate to do justice. The church is mandated to "do justice" to African Americans.

Luke presents the Samaritan parable (Luke 10:29-37) that explicitly details the new meaning of neighbor. Luke does so as a sequel to his version of the double love commandment (love of God;

love of neighbor) in Luke 10:25-28. The actions of the Samaritan attest to a higher proved neighbor to the man who fell among the robbers. He said, "The one who showed mercy on him." And Jesus said to him, "Go and do likewise." (Luke 10:36, 37)

What is Forgiveness?

The reign of God in human affairs means first and foremost that God has taken the initiative to reconcile us, both to God and to each other. Past complicity with the dominating system needs to be acknowledged. Repentance needs to be tendered so that God's forgiveness, already freely given, can be accepted. Old enmities must be healed, for unresolved hatreds can and do lead to acts of revenge.

The political philosopher Hannah Arendt (1984, 18) believes human societies could not exist without forgiveness and the public acts of contrition and confession that make reconciliation possible. Reconciliation is more than forgiveness, however. Forgiveness can be unilateral; reconciliation must be mutual and requires giving something against them. This can be done without their participation. "But reconciliation requires that I and the other person from whom I have been separated by enmity, slavery, racism, and hate mutually forgive each other at a cost[3]."

Forgiveness does not mean that we condone or accept the behavior of the perpetrator. The victim does not turn a blind eye to the crime, but rather frees oneself from ongoing psychological torture, thus clearing a path by which the victim can seek justice that is motivated not by revenge but by the pursuit of universal change and transformation. Harboring enmity and seeking revenge only perpetuates the power of oppressors to lord it over their victims long after the deed was done.

Thus, at the most fundamental level, forgiveness spells liberation for the victim and freedom from guilt for the oppressor. But as Christians, as scholars as churchmen and women, Christian academic institutions and seminaries, we cannot merely stand by

---

3

helplessly. Does not our Christian faith speak of redemption, of liberation, even of forgiveness of enemies? What is forgiveness?

Indeed, because of the pervasiveness of sin and evil, Christian forgiveness must be at once an expression of a commitment to a way of life, the cruciform life of holiness in which we seek to "unlearn" sin and learn the ways of God, and a means of seeking reconciliation amid particular sins, specific instances of brokenness. African Americans need to embody forgiveness for the oppressor to admit ad take ownership of his evil deeds. Thus, reconciliation with justice will be able to take one step forward.

Jones writes in his book "Embodying Forgiveness: A Theological Analysis, (Grand Rapid, MI.: William B. Eerdmans Publishing Company, 1994), forgiveness requires our death, understood in the specific form and shape of Jesus Christ's dying and rising. For as we participate in Christ's dying and rising, we die to our old selves and find a future not bound by the past. "The focus of this dying and rising is the Christian practice of baptism, and it also involves a lifelong practice of living into that baptism, of daily dying to old selves and living into the promise of being embodied new life[4]."

This, at least, is the claim Paul makes in his letter to the Romans. (6:1-11) "What shall we say then? Shall we continue in sin that grace may abound?" (Romans 6:1)

The forgiving grace of Jesus Christ gives people a new perspective on their histories of sin and evil, of their betrayals and they, are being betrayed, of their vicious cycles of being caught as victimizers and victims, so that they can bear to remember the past.

Jones believes the purpose of forgiveness is the restoration of communion, the reconciliation of brokenness. Neither should forgiveness be confined to a word to be spoken, a feeling to be felt or an isolated action to be done; rather, it involves a way of life to be lived in fidelity to God's Kingdom.

Then what is the relationship of baptism to forgiveness? Baptism provides the initiation in God's story of forgiving and reconciling love, definitively embodies in the life, death, and resurrection of Jesus

---

4

of Nazareth. Thus, people are called to embody that forgiveness by unlearning patterns of sin and struggling for reconciliation wherever there is brokenness.

Jones concludes that forgiveness is at once an expression of commitment to a way of life, cruciform life of holiness in which people cast off their old selves and learn to live in communion with God and with one another, and a means of seeking reconciliation amid particular sins, specific instances of brokenness. "In its broadcast context, forgiveness is how God's love moves to reconciliation in the face of sin[5]."

Jones writes Christian forgiveness involves a high cost, both for God and for those who embody it. Further, it requires the discipline of dying and rising with Christ. These disciplines offer no shortcuts to one's giving up possession of oneself. This does not involve self-denial or context of communion is to be restored, love realized reconciliation achieved. African Americans have the courage and spiritual discipline to forgive, and it will be costly. But destiny is calling Africans-Americans for another great sacrifice for humanity.

There are some obstacles, namely, the tendency to see one's own life as something to be either passed or simply given over to another's possession. Consequently, people cling to their power or even their powerlessness.

Dietrich Bonhoeffer (The Communion of Saints, Act and Being, Christ the Center, Creation, and Fall. (1933) argued that Jesus Christ forgives sin through his Person and work. "This is accomplished extra nos (outside us), and as such frees human beings from sin for a new life in Christ[6]."

What Is Reconciliation?

What is Reconciliation? The word, reconciliation, or reconcile, as Paul used it in Greek (katallasso katallage apokattalasso), is not derived from any word in the Hebrew scriptures or Greek religious language.

5
6

"From now on we regard no one according to the flesh; even if we once knew Christ according to the flesh, yet now we know him no longer. So, whoever is in Christ is a new creature; the old things have passed away; behold, new things have come. And all this is from God, who has reconciled us to himself through Christ and given us the ministry of reconciliation with justice namely, God was reconciling the world to himself in Christ, not counting their trespasses against them and entrusting to us the message of reconciliation." (2 Corinthians; 16-19, NAB)

We all share the same Creator (African Americans, Europeans, Asians, Africans, Jews, Greeks, Muslims, and Gentiles). Among the Ten Commandments (Decalogue) of the Old Testament, we recognize the presence of that fifth commandment to honor one's father and mother.

(Exodus 20:12; 21:17; Leviticus 19:3; Deuteronomy 5:16) Jesus himself acknowledged In the New Testament Paul talks about the expediency of being married (I Corinthians 7:9, 28-31), and other New Testament authors give various instructions on the duties of husbands, wives, and children. (Colossians, Ephesians, and I Peter) Besides, the oneness of humanity was illustrated through the creation story of Adam and Eve and their responsibility to procreate.

"Then God blessed them, and God said to them, be fruitful and multiply; fill the earth and subdue it; have dominion over the fish of the sea, over the birds of the air and over every living thing that moves on the earth." (Genesis 1:28)

Scripture does not teach that white men are to have dominion over other races of men/ or over women. Even the United States Constitution reads that all men are created equal and "they have certain inalienable rights, and among these are life, liberty and the pursuit of happiness. "Racism will continue to function despite new legislation. Therefore, new approaches must be implemented to lessen the racial divide in America and the church.

How shall the grandchildren of slaves and the grandchildren of slave owners come to live together in peace? Can peace among races ever be established? Can white Americans achieve their goals without practicing ongoing racism?

How do we come to terms with some of the actors in this tragic drama of racism who do not feel that they have done or are doing no wrong? What do the oppressed who continue to suffer, hurt, and are victimized do when the oppressor does not acknowledge the ownership of their depravity? We are numbered nearly into silence before the enormity of the violence that has been perpetrated upon people just within our lifetime.

Tuesday, September 9, 1997, there was an article in The Daily Times entitled "Cops Hit with New Charges, Plunger Pair Nailed for Bias."

The scripture also teaches, "for we are also his offspring." (Acts 7:28) The bigness of God made a world in which all people are God's offspring. Therefore, God requires that where barriers such as inhumanity, division, racial divide, oppression, and injustice exist, reconciliation with justice must be obtained before people come and offer their gift to God.

The word reconciliation is rooted in scripture. The following passages of scripture contain the word reconciliation or reconcile: II Corinthians 5:7-20, Romans 5:10-11, 11:15; Matthew 5:23-24; Ephesians 2:16; Acts 7:26-28; Colossians 1:20-22; Hebrews 2:17; Luke 23:12; I Corinthians 7:11; Luke 12:58; Genesis 33:4-11; Leviticus 8:15; Daniel 9:24-25 and Ezekiel 45:15.

Paul made it very clear that reconciliation originated with God.

"Therefore, if anyone is in Christ, he is a new creature; old things have passed away: behold, all things have become new. Now all things are of God, who has reconciled us to Himself through Jesus Christ and has given us the ministry of reconciliation. That is, that God was in Christ reconciling the world to Him, not imputing their trespasses to them, and has committed to us the word of reconciliation. "(2 Corinthians 5:17-19)

Reconciliation comes from God, and God has commanded us to be reconciled to our brothers and sisters and God. We are compelled to react to God's initiative in reconciliation, and all humans, including the church, institutions, and nations, are compelled to respond to God's reaching out to us. The process of reconciliation begins when an individual institution accepts God's invitation to make things right.

"For if when we were enemies we were reconciled to God through the death of his Son, much more, having been reconciled, we shall be saved by his life and not only that, but we also rejoice in God through our Lord Jesus Christs, through whom we have now received the reconciliation." (Romans 5:10-11)

The Greek words translated into English as reconciliation (katallasso, katallage, and apikallallasso) were used to describe the results of individuals who had been in opposition to each other becoming friends again. Scripture teaches:

"For it pleases the Father that in Him all the fullness should dwell, and by Him to reconcile all things to Himself, by Him. Whether things on earth or things in heaven, having made peace through the blood of his cross. "Colossians 1:19-20)

Paul says that we were estranged from Good, but through Jesus Christ, we can be reconciled. God invites us demands that we make things right before we come to the altar. (Matthew 5:23-24). Indeed, God's word tells us:

"And you, who once were alienated and enemies in your mind by wicked works, yet now He has reconciled. In the body of his flesh through death, to present you Holy, and blameless, and above reproach in his sight. "(Colossians 1:21-22).

The fullness of life, healing, freedom, and liberation propel us toward wholeness.

However, without restoration (justice) reconciliation is not complete. The man Gabriel, whom Daniel had seen while praying, had come forth to give Daniel skill to understand the vision:

"Seventy weeks are determined for your people and your Holy City to finish the transgression, to make an end of sins, to make reconciliation for the inquiry to bring in everlasting righteousness, "(Daniel, 9:24).

Therefore, reconciliation without justice (righteousness) is not complete, and wholeness is deferred. Reconciliation has three components: being put into friendship with God and each other, radical transformation of a relationship, and restoration of harmony (justice/righteousness).

In the Bible story of Jacob and Esau making peace includes the three components of reconciliation: friendship established, radical change, and transformation of relationship and restoration (justice/righteousness), "But Esau ran to meet him, and embraced him, and fell on his neck and kissed him, and they wept.

Then Esau said, 'What do you mean by all this company which I met?' And he said, 'These are to find favor in the sight of my Lord.' But Esau said, 'I have enough, my brother, keep what you have for yourself.' And Jacob said, 'No, please, if I have now found favor in your sight, then receive my present from my hand since I have seen your face as though I have seen the face of God, and you were pleased with me.

Please, take my blessing that is brought to you, because God has dealt graciously with me and because I have enough.

So, he urged him, and he took it" (Genesis 33:4-11)

Jacob (the oppressor) was compelled to restore Esau (the victim) for the lost inheritance he stole from him. Jacob pleaded with Esau to take what he had stolen from him because he now had favor in the sight of God. Not only favor, but he had seen the face of God, and God was pleased with him. I believe God will be pleased with the church should his church exercise the courage of Jacob and experience the three components of reconciliation.

The Old Testament echoes reconciliation through the word, atonement, God's words teach us to make atonement for them, says the Lord God. (Ezekiel 45:15, Leviticus 8:15) Reconciliation begins with the healing of oppressors through forgiveness, which sparks repentance.

America needs healing; it needs oneness.

Reconciliation cannot be understood without coming to terms with violence and suffering. Such reconciliation is discovered as one becomes tuned through identification with the wounds of Christ to listening and waiting, attention and compassion, and a post-exilic stance. Thereby victims overcome their preoccupation with oppression to become healing agents of reconciliation. How meaningful now becomes the biblical charge that we are not to perform the rituals of our faith while remaining unreconciled to our brother or sister. (Matthew 5:23-24).

This gospel of reconciliation reached out to the powerless in society by transforming the lives of Samaritans, beggars, and others marginalized by society.

The message of reconciliation also reached out to the powerful: An Ethiopian treasury official was baptized, Roman military officers were filled with the Holy Spirit, Roman jailers got saved, and the apostle Paul was on his way to Rome to witness to Caesar himself.

The ministry of reconciliation was brought forth in the world through Jesus's resurrection, and it radically transformed individual lives and cultural environments. The life, death, and resurrection of Jesus Christ ushered in new possibilities for peace and new power for societal transformation. This new possibility for peace has given me a new passion for reconciliation.

We need this passion for reconciliation with justice in Israel between Jews and Palestinians, in Iraq, Iran, and America, as well as in other similar situations.

Sometimes reconciliation may be only an eschatological reality. Nevertheless, the task and the vision predominate like the living water that wells up and flows out of the envisioned temple, bringing refreshment and healing to all. (Ezekiel 47:1-12). The major biblical image of the church is the most developed in the scriptures. In I Corinthians 1:12-13 he states:

"For just as the body, so it is with Christ. For by one Spirit we were all baptized into one body—Jews or Greeks, slaves or free—and all were made to drink of one Spirit."

The image of a human body is applied to the church. We are together as Christ's body, the physical expression of who Jesus is in the world. Christ is the head (Ephesians 4;15), and his life animates and energizes the whole body.

The vision for wholeness and peace, which shines like a beacon of light through the old covenant, gives us important insights into Christian simplicity.

This theme is wonderfully gathered up in the Hebrew word, shalom, a full-bodied concept that resonates with wholeness, unity, and balance. Gathering in (but much broader than) peace, it means a harmonious, caring community with God at its center as the prime sustainer and most glorious inhabitant.

This great vision of Shalom begins and ends our Bible. In the creation narrative God brought order and harmony out of chaos; In the Apocalypse of John, we have the glorious wholeness of a new heaven and a new earth.

The messianic child to be born is to be the prince of peace. (Isaiah 9:6) Justice and righteousness and peace are to characterize his unending kingdom. (Isaiah 9:7) Central to the dream of Shalom is the wonderful vision of all nations streaming to the mountain of the temple of God to be taught godly ways and to walk in godly paths; to beat their swords into plowshares and their spears into pruning hooks. (Isaiah 2:25; Micah 4:1-4) Shalom even carries the idea of a harmonious unity in the natural order: the cow and the bear become friends, the lion, and the lamb lie down together, and a little child leads them. (Isaiah 1:1-9) We are in harmony with God's faithfulness, and loyalty prevails. When we are in harmony with nature; peace and unity reign. The church should work for unity, peace, and reconciliation with justice with African Americans.

Economically and socially, the vision of Shalom is captured in what Bishop John Taylor calls, "The Theology of Enough." The greed of the right is tempered by the need of the poor. -something more freely than equality, more generous than equity, the ever-shifting equipoise of a life system. "Excessive extravagance, vaunting ambition, and ravaging greed—all are foreign to the complete, contended brotherhood of Shalom.

Under the reign of God's Shalom the poor are no longer oppressed, because covetousness no longer rules.

In a particularly tender scene, Jeremiah lamented the fraud and greed of prophet and priest, saying, "They have healed the wound of my people lightly, saying, peace, peace, when there is no peace. (Jeremiah 6:14) In essence, Jeremiah had filed a malpractice suit against the self-styled religious quacks. They had put a Band-Aid over a gaping social wound and said, Shalom, Shalom, all will be well. But Jeremiah thundered, in effect, "In Shalom—all is not well; justice is spurned, the poor oppressed, the orphan ignored. There is no wholeness or healing here!" America's slavery, ongoing racism, its gaping social wound is still open and festering. The pus is seeping out; the odor of systemic racism is stinking. The inhuman lynching is manifesting themselves in rape convictions, police brutality, incarceration, uneven-handed justice to blacks, and subtle racism on African American children.

What Are the Elements of Genuine Reconciliation?

Reconciliation must first take place among Christians, African Americans and whites, Hispanic, Muslims, Asians, and between equals. The evangelical church, so dedicated to foreign missions, has neglected the desperate needs of the inner cities of our own country for too long.

Not only have we neglected the cities, but we have abandoned our transition neighborhoods in Christ to prejudice, racism, and hopelessness.
Declaring that we are all equal without repairing the wrongs of the past is cheap reconciliation. The purpose of repairing wrongs goes beyond the need to restore trust and truth. Reparation should reconstruct the equality of social and economic relationships as well as create a just balance of power within society.

The process of reconciliation begins as we take responsibility for understanding and addressing the discord in society (our community/institutions). Further, we need to repair the wrong done to restore relationships to wholeness.
Genuine reconciliation takes responsibility for disunity and engages in efforts to remove the barriers that exist and restore the original unity intended for the human family.

Forgiveness and reparation are complementary.

Genuine reconciliation must include efforts and strategies to understand the perspective of others. We must remember that although we can empathize, we are not the other person, As we listen we should resist the temptation to believe that we can ever fully know what it is like to be another person or part of a group other than our own.

For example, throughout the dark experience of slavery, African American families were yanked from their native shores and brought to a land where they were strangers.

They were forced to live like animals and expected to breed like cattle. Black males were encouraged to be irresponsible studs that mated and served as beasts, and black women were often molested by masters who forced them to have and rear children that they had no desire to bear.

The encouragement of sexual relationships occurred because slaves were a form of wealth fertility was encouraged for the female slave by cohabitation with male slaves and white plantation owners. It is difficult to overestimate the dismal effects of slavery on family life. The millions of mullatos in America are an indication that white men often force themselves to slave women.

This overwhelming amount of racial mixing is an indication that black culture in America is largely a product of slavery and past slavery patterns. When that fact is coupled with the concept of the black family as "multi-focal," the problems that presently face African American families became more evident. One cannot speak intelligently about the problem of black people in America and not be aware of the historical conditions that have brought about these problems. America's racial divide is largely the price that America must pay for the racist mentalities that produced slavery and for the racist mentalities that continue to practice racism.

According to James Cone, the African American religious experience provides a basis for theological reflection that, unlike most Euro-American religious experiences, is altogether concrete.

African-Americans have developed a spirituality that plants our feet firmly in this earth because the God of our faith demands that we bear witness to the humanity of all by refusing to adapt ourselves to the exploitation that so often the few inflict on the many. The black theology springing from concrete black spirituality has helped black churches to recover the authenticity of their faith so that they will not go wool-gathering in a nebulous kingdom on high and forget their practical responsibility to live obediently in this world, liberating the poor from the misery of poverty.

They are not antithetical—one moves naturally from one to the other in the light of the Christian understanding of God and humanity. The use of the words, liberation, and reconciliation, is deliberate. I speak of freedom instead of liberation. Cone believes liberation is revolutionary—for blacks it points to what might be. Black Christians desire radical and rapid social change in America as a matter of survival. Black theology is a theology of liberation. Therefore, we believe the Christian faith is avowedly revolutionary and may speak to this need with great force.

J. Deotis Roberts believes reconciliation is also crucial and there is a theological basis for this reconciliation between equals.

I am impressed by the first words from Mr. Joe Sacramone, now director of Land Claims Court Government of South Africa. His witness to justice led to imprisonment and torture. He tells us in an interview, "It is through reconciliation that we regain our humanity. To work for reconciliation is to live to show others what their humanity is." I hope that we can take his advice.

The second is from Frantisek Cardinal Temasek, the Roman Catholic Primate of Czechoslovakia, who was ninety years old at the downfall of the communist regime in 1989. fearlessly for over two decades. In Christianity Today, his public address to the people of Czechoslovakia after freedom came, he said "Let us fight for the good with good means!

We have seen in our oppressors the short-lived victory of male violence, of hatred, of revenge, of ruthlessness and arrogance." Those are the words of someone who has tasted reconciliation.

Reparation

What is Reparation? Reparations mean to repair, to make whole again. The double consciousness of Americans of African descent first described by W.E.B. DuBois, the age-old chasm between our identification with this country and our cultural affinity toward the black diaspora and Africa cannot be bridged until there is a final rendezvous with our history.

Therefore, ultimately, that the demand for black reparations is not fundamentally about the money. The rape victim does not press charges and goes to court simply to receive financial compensation. The rape victim desires and demands that the truth should be told about the crime. The Jewish survivors and their descendants of the Holocaust in Europe during World War II, and the Armenian people who experienced mass genocide under the Turkish Ottoman Empire in World War I am not motivated primarily by financial restitution. Victims want the public record to reflect what happened.

Oppressed people live their lives in a kind of state-imposed traumatic existence when the criminality and violence hurled against us is rarely acknowledged. We are presented to the world by our racists' oppressors as being people outside of history, devoid of a past of any consequence. To heal the effects of trauma our stories must be told and retold. The oppressed thus perceive themselves in a new and liberating way. They can now, at long last, become actors and exercise agency at the vanguard of a new history. The divided double consciousness becomes a greater, critical, and truer consciousness, creating the capacity to speak with clarity and confidence about oneself and the totality of society. As W.EB. Dubois wrote in 1903: "The history of the American Negro is the history of this strife—this longing to attain self-conscious manhood, to merge his double self into a better and truer self."

Therefore, reparation means making amends, compensation, repairing wrongs that one caused (directly or indirectly). "Reparation must reconstruct the equality of social and economic injustice and create a balance of power within society[7]."

Community

What is Community? A community is a place where you can come and be yourself and have the same value that you have or that my

---

[7]

neighbor has, regardless of that person's color or lifestyle preference. In that place, we have the same value as everybody else, and I can feel the freedom to express my opinion without embarrassment or without feeling that I am overstepping my bounds. Community is something more than the sum of its parts, its members. The seeds of the community reside on the earth. But it is not a gem while in the rough; it is simply as a stone. "Therefore, a group becomes a community in somewhat the same way that a stone becomes a gem—through a process of cutting and polishing[8]." Once cut and polished, it is something beautiful.

But to describe its beauty, the best we can do is to describe its facets. Community is multi-faceted, each facet a mere aspect of a whole that defies description.

The community has several facets:

Community is inclusive
Community is realistic
Community is healing and converting
Community is a Spirit
Community is a safe place
Community has four stages
    Pseudo community
    Chaos
    Emptiness
    Community

Community Develops in Response to Crisis

Community is a state of being together, in which people, instead of hiding behind their defenses, learn to lower them, in which instead of attempting to obliterate their differences people learn not only to accept them but rejoice in them. Therefore, the key to community is acceptance of the celebration of our individual and

---

[8]

cultural differences, overcoming racism and becoming one through reconciliation is mandatory.

What is Fellowship

A fellowship is a group of persons with a common interest. Among Christians, the common bond is their faith in Christ, particularly in partaking in the Lord's Supper. Jesus gave us a clear promise in John 17:20-23: non-Christians will be able to recognize believers as did Jesus' disciples because of the love for each other. "The church should seek the holism that is included by Professor Ron Sider in his book, One-Sided Christianity,36 which speaks to Shalom, wholeness, completeness, and inclusiveness[9]."

Throughout the Bible, God restates the oneness of humanity. "And God said to Noah, this is the sign of the covenant which I have established between me and all flesh that is on the earth. Now the sons of Noah who went out of the ark were Shem, Ham, and Japheth. And Ham was the father of Canaan. These three were the sons of Noah, and from these, the whole earth was populated." (Genesis 9:17-19)

The author is convinced of the fact that this oneness is recorded by the Hebrew writers of the Bible gives further evidence that, even as they developed their own ethnic identity, they recognized that the Hebrew people belonged to a larger human family. Scripture teaches that God has "made from one blood every nation of men to dwell on all the face of the earth and has determined their reappointed times and the boundaries of their dwellings." (Acts 17:26)

In the Delaware Times, Wednesday, September 17, 1997, an article was entitled. "Racial Remarks Spur Boycott Call."

This kind of remark has been made to African Americans in the church. Whoever hired Ganglia has a blurred vision of humanity. This is subtle racism at its greatest and ignorance at the highest level of academia. There is no wholeness or healing, shalom is not well. Part of understanding the other's truth is feeling his or her pain.

---

[9]

Taking responsibility means feeling the pain of isolation, tokenisms, inferiority, fear, and anger. The powerful must feel the pain of the powerless. The victimizer must feel the pain of the vulnerable. Men must understand how women are affected by sexism and how sexism may shape their view of men. Whites need to understand the painful effects of racism on persons of color and grasp how this may affect the perception of whites.

But the healing peace of God will not be spurned forever. Isaiah's son saw a day when the reconciliation between people will be a reality, a day when justice and righteousness will reign, a time when the wholeness of God's peace will rule, and people will "walk in the light of the Lord, "(Isaiah 2:4-5) I believe it's time for America to reconcile for slavery, Jim Crow, sharecropping, lynching, unequal and separate and the ongoing, systemic racism and failed affirmative-action program.

America has inflicted wounds upon African American people and has failed to take ownership of its inhumane, evil acts.

The odor of racism is stinking; the wound cannot heal if the pulse (the root causes) goes unaddressed. The churches' racist behavior and ongoing practices toward African Americans prevent America from becoming whole and experiencing Shalom. Further, the churches' racist behavior robs African-Americans and whites of the ability to experience "the whole gospel for the whole through whole persons. When you allow barriers to existing it prevents America from becoming whole. When the church places barriers in African Americans' path who is at fault?

Certainly not African American.

Therefore, we realize a tragic deed in the sight of God and humanity has been done by the church.

What is the strength of the church?

"It seeks to equip persons for Christian ministry who view that ministry who view that ministry as a divine vocation, who know themselves to be called by God and are committed to growing toward wholeness in their relationship with God, self, others, and their world[10]." The church is committed to assist persons toward:

An awareness of their brokenness and dependence upon God
The development of a spirit of openness toward others in the global body of Christ, beginning with an appreciation of that body's expression in the diverse Christian community in America
A disciplined devotional life, bearing fruit in a vital, growing, contagious faith.
Regular participation in worship and fellowship, which supports faith, expands vision, furthers intimacy with God and others, and increases awareness of the presence and power of the Holy Spirit.

Is it right for African Americans to be denied the reality of the church's mission? Is it the intent of the church's leadership to continue this practice? In an especially poignant passage, scripture brings together the three Hebrew concepts we have studied: justice, compassion, and peace. The psalmist points to the day when "Steadfast love and faithfulness will meet; righteousness and peace will kiss each other." (Psalm 85:10)

Peter Paris, in his book, Overcoming Alienation in Theological Education, "Shifting Boundaries: Contextual Approaches to the Structure of Theological Education writes that the civil-rights struggle gave rise to an insistence on the access of African Americans to white institutions.[11]" In the church, however, he states, no serious thought has been given to how those institutions might be significantly altered by the African American presence.

Consequently, few schools have given thought to the necessity of reforming themselves to meet the needs of African Americans, and virtually none have thought seriously about reciprocal benefits that would be derived from the interracial association.

"Christian theology traditionally has maintained through the church that the truth of the Christian faith is a truth appropriate

---

10
11

to all people in all manner of circumstances[12]." This theological universalism has promoted the cultural imperialism of Western, white-male thought. It has obscured distinctive social or ethnic contexts, and it has marginalized numerous groups of people. African Americans have been marginalized by the church.

12

CHAPTER VI

Introduction

The Urgency of the Model

Racial attitudes in America appear to be reflected in its institutions (Legislative, Executive and Judicial) and leadership, and inhibiting racial reconciliation with justice and sidelining exploding Diversity. To date, there are more than five million children born from diverse families in America. Racism, as a contemporary phenomenon has historical roots and has inflicted historical pain and suffering, which must be overcome to empower Christian leaders, educators, and the church for reconciliation with justice. The reality of institutional racism in the church toward African Americans and other minority communities makes new, approaches necessary for a resolution to develop structures for sustaining and nurturing a network of trained church-based advocates skilled in cross-cultural communication.

The purpose is to develop a model to empower Christian leaders to take on new roles as effective agents of reconciliation with justice and peacemakers in their churches and communities. This project model will provide training in reconciliation, mediation, proactive peacemaking, and cross-cultural communication. It intends further to focus on the transformation of an institution. The design seeks to create leaders in the area of personal, congregational, community, and global transformation. The church/government as an institution can experience transformation and renewal, especially as it pertains to historical racism, so that in the end it may become a more effective institution while learning to manage its diversity.

Ideally, the model can be replicated at other theological institutions. There are several features of the proposed model.

The first component is the establishment of the Institutional Support Group. This ISG will be selected from the lay leadership of the church. The ISG will journey with the author through this project. They will:

Support the ministry leader's involvement in the program
Help evaluate their institution's ministry needs
Assist in guiding the ministry leader in designing the required
    Renewal project that is to benefit the institution
Provide counsel and support to the ministry leader as needed, and
Provide performance evaluation of the ministry leader at intermittent
    stages and the conclusion of the program.

The model suggests that for the church to empower adequately its members as peacemakers, it must first reconcile itself as an institution. The Black Church was born in a fundamentalist era blighted with slavery, lynching, and racism, evidenced by the treatment of African Americans since 1619. The writer suggests diversity as a solution to this blight and illustrates the institution's struggle to change over the years. However, America is hemorrhaging, and white males' fundamental right to free speech is challenged.

The Urgency to Overcome Racism

The evils of racism have been addressed on many levels and from many angles. However, the subject of the urgency in addressing racism is somewhat unique. Indeed, much of what is written on the broader subject can lead us to conclude that the pervasiveness of racism and its systemic nature renders any near-term solution unattainable. From this comes a complacency that will undermine a sense of urgency in the fight against this evil. Therefore, this topic is timely and important. The author will begin by addressing the root cause of racism and draw us to the reasons why we must act with a sense of urgency in our battle.

The author will conclude with a few comments on the steps we might take as we press on in this important and urgent work.

Root Causes of Racism

A misunderstanding of the root causes of racism can lead to the complacency we mentioned above Such a misunderstanding can also lead us astray in our effort to combat racism and make our best-intentioned efforts ineffectual. Therefore, let us be clear about the basis for racism that we might understand just as clearly the way it must be overcome.

As Christians, our worldview generally begins in one and only one place, in the person of Jesus Christ.

Christ came to reveal to us the heart, the very nature of God. In that self-revelation, Jesus also shows us who we are, and from this new self-understanding, we then make the ethical decisions about how we are to live. The methodology for our ethical decisions must always have this clear direction. It begins with our knowing our God in Jesus Christ. It continues with us knowing who we are as children of this God. It concludes with our ethical choices based on this dual understanding. With this methodology in place, we see first that God revealed to us in Jesus Christ is a triune God, a God in a relationship. The Godhead of Father, Son, and Holy Spirit was and is revealed to us in Jesus Christ, in this self-revelation we learn that God's nature is gracious, holy, merciful, and righteous. We learn that this God is for us, that we were created to be in fellowship with this God, that this God calls us into a right relationship with him, and with a father eagerly looking down the road for the return of the prodigal son, this God waits for us to return to him. The God we know in Jesus Christ is this loving, righteous, triune God whose very nature is relational. Scripture goes on to tell us that we were created in the image and likeness of this God. That is, we were created in the image of the Trinitarian God, a God defined by a mutual indwelling, by fellowship, by relationship. From this teaching about the Imago

Dei, we are confronted with a basic reality about our own created nature. Simply put, we are created for relationships. We find our completion in a relationship. We know our greatest contentment in a relationship. We glorify God most completely in a relationship.

How else could we live if we have been created in the image of a triune God? How else could we live if we have been saved by the blood of the one who came to bring us back into fellowship with this God? How else could we live if we have been led by the Spirit into an ongoing life of communion with fellow believers so that our unity might be our greatest witness to this God? This relationship can be seen on four levels: first in our relationship to God, Second in our relationship to ourselves, third in our relationship to one another, and fourth in our relationship to creation. The Christian life is a life lived in and for Christ on all four levels.

There is a second aspect of our world view that arises here. It emerges from the fall. If we have defined our created state correctly, then we will also see that the fall was a denunciation of and quickly a deterioration of our relationships at every level. It began with Adam and Eve hiding from the God they now feared. It continued with their awareness that they were naked, which now meant separation rather than completion. It spread to their mutual accusations, and thus began the history of humanity's hatred and strife. It culminated in their brokenness with the much-created world that was put in place just for their pleasure.

When we speak about our world view, we can only do so from outside the gates of Eden. Therefore, our perception is always prone to distortion and manipulation.

However, we must not miss the central truth that we were created for healthy, whole, and joyous relationships at all four levels, and that the fall brought brokenness into all four.

Now we can see the root cause of racism.

For racism to exist there must be either ignorance or an outright denial of the Father that was revealed to us in the Son by the power of the Spirit. To be racist we must believe that we are someone other than the child and creation of the triune God of grace. We must believe that God is some other god than the Father of the Christ of Calvary, or we must believe in no god at all! When we see God in Jesus Christ, we see our common state before God; we see our common falseness, our common need for grace, and our common utter lostness. We do not stand above or below our brother or sister in this place. We all stand as broken and in need of grace.

Consequently, in Jesus Christ, we also see our common redemption. We, as His redeemed children, can only see our brothers and sisters of every race and kind as like us and with us, rescued together from our sinfulness by the grace of God. The root cause of racism is the sin of ignorance—ignorance of who God is, and the resulting ignorance of which we are as the creation of God. Such ignorance is an active sin. This is aggressive ignorance. It is not just the absence of knowledge but the denial of truth. It is a determined effort to turn away from the truth in the fear that the truth might change us. And of course, it will. So, we shove it to the side, argue it away, or pretend it just does not apply to this situation. And the seed of racism becomes planted in the fertile soil of the ignorance that comes from the denial of truth.

Racism, then, is the ultimate form of self-deception. The one who cannot see his brother or sister as equal cannot see himself as Jesus sees him.

The woman who believes she is better than her sister has lost her identity as the child of the God who believed in her to the point of death on a cross. Therefore, the Old Testament speaks so harshly against idolatry.

Similarly, idolatry is a denial of our created state before God. When we create false gods, we deny the reality of the true God, and thus, we deny our very identity as children of God. We can see the parallels between idolatry and racism; both lead to a denial of the essence of our humanity, and thus, both are self-deception and delusion.

The root cause of racism is a deep sickness in our souls. When we deny our very essence, we breed brokenness at every other level of our existence. We cannot be in the right fellowship with God, ourselves, our neighbor, or creation if we do not know who we are. Therefore, racism is so destructive. It steals first our self-understanding, and it spreads like a virus into every other area of our life, until the image of the relational God is wiped from our lives.

The Urgency of Our Fight

It is popular to believe that racism is only a tangential sin that, if left alone, will not affect the rest of our lives. This is especially true for so many in our churches who do not consider themselves to be "racist" because they have never engaged in outward acts of a racist nature.

They shrug off the internal biases and prejudices they may have, and they leave unconfronted the stereotypes they employ every day, believing that none of this is problematic. Without knowing it, they give a welcome place to the virus that will devour their soul.

Racism is self-deception, and that self-deception will work its way through the entirety of our being like a virus through the body, multiplying and spreading. It cannot do otherwise. When we lose our self-identity as children of the triune God of grace, we lose also the ability for the Spirit of God to transform us more into the image of that God.

What is at stake is not merely our ability to relate interracially, but our ability to be Christ-like in any area of our life. For this reason, overcoming racism must have the utmost urgency to our church and personal transformation.

We can add to this urgency by looking at three specific aspects of racism, namely, that it is destructive because the enemy we fight is, by nature, a destroyer. When we allow the soul-sickness of racism a place in our life, we invite in a destroyer and initiate a process that has the potential to wreak havoc in our relationships. Racists find no peace in themselves or their relationships with others and certainly not with their creator. This may not happen all at once, but slowly, as a place is given for an enemy of our souls to work in us, it will happen. If we respond to racism with apathy or complacency, we buy time for this cancer to spread. Our response to this virus must be immediate and potent. To shrink back from action is to yield our souls to further effects of this insidious, destructive force.

Persistent recurrences of racial incidents and the public debate over affirmative action continue to engage the American consciousness with the question of race. The 1992 riots in the wake of the verdict in the Rodney King beating trial were the signs of fracturing (recurring virus). Varying reactions to the O.J. Simpson trial verdict revealed the differences in perspective black and white Americans generally possess. "Both cases stirred anger, hostility, destructiveness, sickness, and resentment across racial lines[13]."

Racism is also systemic, which ought to call us to immediate and sustained action. Every day that a sick and destructive system is left unattended, the evil in it becomes further entrenched and more deeply embedded. And this can be said for our third area as well.

The fact that racism is generational should be the clearest indication of why we must have great urgency in our work.

Millions of young minds are being polluted every day by parents, peers, and a societal system that preaches, or at least accommodates racism. As a new generation of soul-sick men and women take places of responsibility and power, the system continues, and the forces for evil remain, and we are guaranteed that the next generation will follow suit. According to recent data released by the U.S. Census Bureau, racial disparities in education, income, and homeownership persist and in some cases are still growing.

Many Americans see racism as a lingering problem. Polls show blacks more than twice as likely to call racism a "very serious" problem, and almost half of whites and blacks say they know someone racist.

Persistent recurrences of racial incidents are intensifying and becoming an epidemic. In 2007 we saw the demise of Don Imus, former talk-show host, after his derogatory and racist statement on national airwaves, calling the Rutgers women basketball team "nappy-headed hoes" on the air. The NCAA released this statement: "The NCAA and Rutgers University are offended by the insults on MSNBC's Don Imus program. It is unconscionable that anyone would use the airwaves to utter such disregard for the dignity of human beings. Racism is like a virus that has mutated into a new

---

13

form that we don't recognize." The Imus virus has spread and infected the New York City Police Department.

Tuesday, April 24, 2007, three female NYPD officers accuse the sergeant of using racist, sexist remarks during roll call.

Changing systems and breaking generational patterns are extremely hard. Yet without such changes, racism will not be overcome. This should motivate us to the highest state of urgency.

Every new generation offers a fresh opportunity to start breaking generational patterns. Every transfer of power is a moment in history to educate and empower those who can lead us out of the darkness into His marvelous light.

We have no time to waste. The virus is active and powerful. The stakes could not be higher. The battle must be engaged and sustained. And the victory is already assured, for scripture proclaims, "Greater is He that is in us, than he that is in the world." If we are convinced of the urgency in the battle against racism, what might be our solution? First, there must be a return to the Word of God. It is simply a fact that churches that commit themselves to study and following God's Word will be confronted with their racism and will seek to change. Biblical illiteracy and biblical apathy are forerunners of racism in the church.

When we decide to commit ourselves to know and obey God's Word, we will have taken the first step in this battle.

Second, we must articulate clearly why racism is so destructive and why this battle must have such urgency.

Until people understand the insidious nature of racism and its connection with the whole of our lives as Christians, we will be hard-pressed to move it to the front burner of the church's agenda. This story must be told.

Finally, we must decide on our role and begin to act. Every Christian can and must take personal responsibility in the battle against racism.

Whether it is praying over our attitudes that must be changed, working in our churches to replace ignorance with understanding, participating in some form of political action, writing a politician, talking to our children, or reading a book to better understand this issue, we all must find our role in this battle. And we must begin today.

Let us commit ourselves to this critical work. Let us be sources of understanding in the face of ignorance. Let us give no place in our souls to the enemy. Let us name our racist attitudes and repent that we might be a vessel that God can use to bring transformation to others. Let us be shaken from our complacency and inspired to action for the sake of the God who came in His Son that we might have life and have it abundantly.

If racism is a denial of our very identity as children of a loving, triune God, then nothing can be more urgent than its defeat.

CHAPTER VII

Embracing Diversity and Differences can unify our nation to become one.

I am here today, fellow Rotarians, to offer you a new possibility for how we conduct our affairs, both on a personal and on a societal level. I am here to renew the possibility of our United States truly becoming one both on a person-to-person level.

For, if this great experiment in Democracy is going to reach its full potential in our nation, we must truly face our differences and our choices and our diversity...and then RISE ABOVE THEM!

Rise above them and recognize that our differences... differences in culture, differences in affluence, differences in skill sets, differences in thought...are indeed our strength. We must explore this possibility before the divide becomes too great.

Exploring the Possibilities

I believe in the possibility of our nation unifying on our way to Becoming One. The possibility of our nation embracing our differences and our diversity and the possibility of unlocking the true and full potential of these United States of America.

Our nation has done great things.

Through a convergence of hard work, innovation, faith, and divine providence, America has been and remains. THE beacon of hope throughout the rest of the world.

Yet, internally…within our nation, this divide that we don't just know, but that we feel, does limit us. Our potential as a nation has been shackled and represent and even strategically ignored in favor of these false dichotomies that have pervaded public discourse and policy formation and even our town, our state, and our nation most recently.

Now, you may be sitting there in front of me, right now wondering. Wondering "How in the world do you expect me to believe that embracing diversity and differences can unify our nation to become one?" Don't differences, just on their surface, result in the division?

Don't differences by their very nature mean that we are not unified? How could differences be a UNIFYING force in America?

After all, aren't there bound to be different opinions, values, and motives ALL mashed up together in this diversity salad that we are striving for? How could this possibly be a template for Becoming One?

And I will tell you that these concerns are valid. They are true. And they are heartfelt by almost everyone who considers them. And, by themselves, these differences will AND HAVE divided us.

Black-White Problem Is Now Multi-Ethnic

The Black-white problem has become multi-ethnic. We are experiencing rapid change in our country and the church, rapid mixing of our communities in which the issues of race-, culture-, and gender diversity cause us many times to turn on each other rather than toward one another. It is very difficult for many of us, as we look at the rapid change in our communities, to begin to understand what it all means, where we fit, how we relate, and how we can begin to develop community.

Since the black-white problem is now multi-ethnic, how do we deal with racism in this broad context without dealing at the same time with the fundamental historical/contemporary black-white conflict? The conventional assumption that the United States is a melting pot and that, therefore, we ought all to become an amalgam was predicated upon the assumption that everybody should be like the Euro-American and should adapt to their culture and negate or place their own culture in the second status. There was no assumption that white Americans should learn to appreciate other cultures or languages, especially African Americans. To white America, African Americans had nothing to contribute to the community except their slave labor and ability to entertain white folk (for example, with sports and music). That is no longer an operative assumption.

Today white Americans must come to terms with the whole concept of diversity, which has resulted in a plethora of experiences. The multi-cultural realities of urban existence and in the church have forced the leadership in America and the church to a new appreciation and new understanding of the story of the day of Pentecost.

First, certain other assumptions and paradigms must change. The way we understand our political system and our appreciation for political diversity will be one of the most entrenched prejudices against which we will have to struggle if we are to address adequately the opportunity to embrace the diversity that is now upon us. What do I mean by that? One of the things I have come to understand as I prepare to travel to South Africa as a Plowshare Fellow is that we in the United States probably are the most parochial, limited, culturally deprived nation on the globe in our political and racial outlook. We expect everyone else to live, think, speak, act, look, buy, and behave in the ways we do. What arrogance this nation flaunts! That clearly must change.

We assume that our own political and economic systems are one of the gifts that God has mandated us to give to the world. The truth is that our systems are the most effective fertilizer for the growth of myths, prejudices, cultural insensitivities, and racism that can attend us as we seek to face this challenging moment for change in the direction of multi-culturalism and reconciliation with justice with African-Americans.

Diversity is no longer a phenomenon happening exclusively in New York, Philadelphia, Chicago, and Los Angles.

It is a foretaste of what is going to be happening in every small community in America. It is a reality that is with us now. It is just an urban reality; it is the reality of America and the church. It is the reality we must learn to address, dialogue about, benefit from, and celebrate.

The church can become a model for Americans and every community and institution in America. However, it must first right the wrongs that were done to African Americans. The church must practice the willing suspension of its belief in some of the paradigms and world views that have been the ways of thinking and acting about African Americans, and that is a hard thing to do. The church must embrace the same laws the nation embraces to eliminate racism. It is hard to respect other people operating with the assumption that the church has.

To overcome the barriers to diversity and to build bridges, the church must begin by determining where we are.

That is, we need to identify who we are and how we think. Let me suggest some diversity terms on an awareness spectrum and ask that you look at them, figure out where you are, and maybe, where your church is.

That is the challenge before the church in America. But there is hope, and I find that hope in scripture I find that hope in what God did in one of the great miracles recorded in the New Testament. At Pentecost, the beginning of the new church, God used multi-culturalism to break through the prejudices and limited thinking of those who had come into the early church. They believed that the rest of the world should be like them and suddenly they found that this new experience was a multi-cultural experience. I pray to God that our experience in the church in America will be as world-shaking.

Reinhold Niebuhr

White Americans and African Americans have not yet learned how to live together without compounding their vices and covering each other with mud and with blood. Reconciliation with justice is our only hope of making progress in solving the problems of the racial divide. Whatever the cost, it is less costly than the parting of more blood.

The author believes the society in which each person lives is at once the basis for, and the nemesis of, that fullness of life that each person seeks. I believe in the whole gospel for the whole world through the whole people.

However, where racism is practiced, I cannot be whole, nor can the individuals who practice racism.

The cost of practicing reconciliation may mean that we consider the needs of others even when they compete with our own. To use our reconciling gifts, we need to be visionaries and activists. As visionaries, we learn to recognize separation and oppression while we develop our comprehension of the multiple causes of injustice. Additionally, we seek to understand how injustice produces long-term oppression.

Then we can understand what creates a just society, and we embrace the role of the activist by devising and executing processes for moving away from the way things are and genuine belief that conditions actually can improve that he/she inspires others to labor for transformation.

Robert Briffault, in his Rational Evolution, makes a convincing analysis of this function of reason in the attainment of justice.

Racism in the church must be recognized for what it is. This study is not designed to destroy the social prestige of the church in the community by revealing the relationship between the special privileges of the majority and the misery of the underprivileged. Nor is it not intended to limit their ability to assert their interests and protect their special privileges with the same degree of self-deception. However, its focus is to raise the conscious level of the church for self-examination, and to undergo a personal transformation, thus enabling the institution to embrace reconciliation with justice.

Reconciliation with justice is a citadel of hope for the church and America's racial divide, which is on the edge of despair. The resources and the limitation of religion in dealing with social problems are revealed more clearly in its spirit of love than in its sense of contribution.

To embrace reconciliation with justice is costly. The church ay must risk losing its conservative benefactors and discontinue its subtle practice of racism. The church must change its evangelistic outreach and focus on African Americans transitioning into their community. The decrease in church closures would positively impact transition neighborhoods.

CHAPTER VIII

What we all share and what we all have in Common

Yet there is a key element here that we may not be considering. What is it in these United States of America that we ALL share? What do we have IN COMMON? How, in fact, are we all THE SAME?

These are the questions that motivated two of our nation's pillars 50 years ago back in 1968 when Dr. Martin Luther King and Attorney General Robert Kennedy were leading their efforts towards America Becoming One.

Reverend King was a self-proclaimed "Dreamer." He dreamed that "little black boys and black girls will be able to join hands with little white boys and white girls as sisters and brothers." And there are signs that his dream has come true. Just look around and look at who is holding hands, who are dating, who are getting married, who are having children? Have you gone to the public/private schools, colleges/universities lately? What do you see? Further, have you looked in your family lately? Black/White, Hispanic/White, Hispanic/Black, Philippines/Black, German/Black. These folks have put their differences aside and have Become One.

Bobby Kennedy too was keenly interested in the underprivileged in our nation, but, rather than being a Dreamer, like King, Bobby's efforts were strongly rooted. Like many of you here, Bobby knew that the road to Becoming One and the truly United States of America is extremely difficult.

REV. DR. ALBERT R. REDDICK

Research: All Black men killed by police officers,' all white men killed by police officers, All Black women in prison, all white women in prison, all black children born in prison, and All White children born in prison.

CHAPTER IX

Moral Courage is a rarer commodity than bravery in battle or great intelligence

Kennedy laid down the harshness of our challenge when he mused, "Few men are willing to brave the disapproval of their peers, the censure of their colleagues, the wrath of their society. Moral courage is a rarer commodity than bravery in battle or great intelligence. Yet it is the one essential, vital quality for those who seek to change a world that yields most painfully to change." "Intelligence is the ability to adapt to change" (Stephen Hawking).

Moral courage? Moral courage! As you sit there wondering how we can achieve this courage enough to resist disapproval by my peers and the wrath of society?

Both men did have moral courage, as they were tragically silenced by the disapproval of their peers and the wrath of society. BUT…their legacy still lingers today! The rippling effects of Dr. King and Bobby Kennedy continue to drive our debate, motivate us, and force us to face the reality that, despite the incredible progress we've made at Becoming One, there is still more work to be done.

Martin Luther King on The Power of Love

Despite his historical background, Martin developed a deep capacity to love people.

Though deeply committed to a program of freedom for African Americans, he had a love and deep concern for all ethnic groups.

Martin through the power of the Holy Spirit, spoke to America about war and peace, social justice and racial discrimination, about its obligation to the poor, and about non-violence. Martin embraced non-violence but not fear or cowardice. He embraced non-violence out of moral courage and challenged the inter-racial injustice of his country without a gun. He had the faith to believe that he would win the battle for justice.

Martin Luther King, Jr. had the message of Jesus Christ, and he used the method of Mahatma Gandhi. Gandhi challenged the British Empire without a sword and won, Martin challenged the racism and injustice in America without a gun. He was a devout believer in Jesus Christ and the power of Jesus' love.

Bishop Thomas Hoyt (1977, 12-15) examined the influence of the poverty message of the Old Testament upon Kings' exegesis.

Hoyt believes that King came to black people and brought a message of hope to the poor and the oppressed in the language they knew well.

Hoyt believes King saw the scripture as providing archetypical experiences that were conducive to understanding the times. King's method was to retell the story that would force the oppressors to hear again the sound of freedom and cause the oppressed to experience hope and motivation for the pursuance of freedom.

Therefore, Hoyt believed that King helped us understand that God identifies with and empowers the powerless and that the Bible is relevant to political theory and practice.

King believed in the unity of the Bible. For him, the God of Amos was also the God of Jesus. He also had a holistic understanding of persons. Throughout his public career, Martin Luther King, Jr. was criticized because the non-violence protests, he led often generated violence. King knew well that "the peaceful demonstration he organized would bring tough repressive measures by the police."

Critics misunderstood non-violence to be passive and submissive. On the contrary, it is an active and often disruptive method of resisting injustice and bringing about social change. A Gandhi explained, non-violence does not mean meek submission to the will of the evildoer, but it means the pitting of one's whole soul against the will of the tyrant. Working under this law of our being, a single individual can defy the whole might of an unjust empire. Moreover, non-violence is often coercive, applying physical and moral pressure to force opponents to bargain. James Farmer of CORE believes that where we cannot influence the heart of the evildoer, we can force an end to the evil practice.

The strategy of non-violence operates by what has been termed a moral form of jiu-jitsu.

Skillfully applied, non-violence action throws the opponent off balance, causing his violence to rebound against him, weakening his moral position. For this moral jiu-jitsu to work, opponents must be provoked to commit their violence openly so that it may be widely exposed. Whenever racists responded to non-violence with violence in the presence of the media, they undermined their support among uncommitted third parties and added legitimacy to the protesters' call. Racists have learned from King's non-violence movement how to control and subdue their racist behavior. Therefore, subtle racism has come into existence. It is controlled, subdued, and carefully manipulated. It is more deadly than the fire hoses, dogs, and midnight riders of the KKK. It consists of such practices as hire a female rather than an African American male, hires a Hispanic rather than an Afro-American, and hire a Caribbean or African who looks like African Americans. Therefore, the public image is placated with the appearance that an African American is on board.

Dr. King was inclined to stress the importance of converting racists by reason and persuasion. Through non-violence, he believed African Americans would eventually change the hearts of their racist oppressors. The student sit-ins of 1960 and the Freedom Riders of 1961, which forced Southern racists to comply with federal law—

taught King that non-violent direct action must rely more upon conflict and coercion, even at the price of provoking violence from white racists. As King wrote in his letter from Birmingham jail, we have not made a single gain in civil rights without determined legal and nonviolent pressure. Moreover, non-violent direct action was the catalyst that compelled the federal government to act and the federal courts to render decisions in support of civil rights.

Through experience, King perceived that love and reconciliation would not succeed in overturning segregation without the power of non-violent direct action.

According to King, Reinhold Niebuhr said: "Powerless goodness ends upon the cross." Without power, love is ineffective, and without love, power is liable to become abusive and violent. As King explained (Childress), power at its best "is love implementing the demands of justice." When employed on a mass scale, non-violence is the most potent method for oppressed people to overcome their oppression.

King called for a realization that a power not rooted in love is reckless and abusive while a love devoid of power is sentimental and anemic. Inspired by Tillich's theme of the union of love, power, and justice King maintained: "Power at its best is love implementing the demands of justice. Justice at its best is love correcting everything that stands against love."

Scripture teaches,

"But I say to you, love your enemies, bless those who curse you, do good to those who hate you and pray for those who spitefully use you and persecute you." (Matthew 5:44)

Confronted with this critique of the value of love from social good, King believed that Jesus' ethical messages of:

"Turn the other cheek and love your enemies are effective only in conflicts among individuals but are not useful in resolving conflicts among racial groups and nations."

King's original faith in the power of love was evident throughout his struggle for change in America. In "I Have a Dream" King maintained that the Christian virtues of love, mercy, and forgiveness should stand at the center of our lives. There is the danger that those of us who have lived so long under the yoke of oppression, those of us who have been exploited and trampled over, those of us who have had to stand amid the tragic midnight of injustice and indignities will enter the new age with hate and bitterness. But if we retaliate with hate and bitterness, the new age will be nothing but a duplication of the old age.

King believed love would be the salvation of our civilization, and he was impressed with the motto "Freedom and Justice through love," not through violence: not through hate; no, not even through boycotts; but through love.

The racial divide in this nation caused by its dehumanizing, enslavement of Africans and African Americans since 1619 still represents one of the most oppressive, barbaric, sinful, ungodly acts perpetrated against God's beings.

African Americans continue to be depersonalized cogs in a vast racist system. We are merely property subject to the dictates of white America. The loud noises just a few days ago from the legislative halls of the South in interposition and nullification, we hear from the West and North: "Reverse discrimination; down with affirmative action."

The death groans of an old system of slavery, lynching, Jim Crow, and separate but unequal continue to grow and refuse to die. Racism is alive and continues to rule the day.

However, major changes have occurred since the civil rights struggle that demands this nation's and African Americans' most careful observation. America's population has shifted from primarily two ethnic groups: African Americans who built the nation and supplied the labor force also dared to love their oppressors despite their inhuman enslavement.

We must ask the question; can we continue to fight for affirmative action as we know it?

Can we continue to seek integration as we know it? I believe we are at the end of America. A boycott although not an end within itself, is no longer a means to awaken a sense of shame within the oppressors and challenge their false sense of superiority.

The dynamics of the multi-cultural and the racial-diversity explosion that has occurred in America challenges African Americans to rise above the narrow confines of our individualistic concerns to the broader concerns of all humanity. The new world is a global world of geographical linkage where all people intermingle and impact each other. Computer technology has created our information age that discloses the weakness and strengths of nations accessing the information highway. This means that no individual, no ethnic group nor nation can live alone or force its culture upon another. Can we continue to seek to integrate the staff of our urban schools when forced busing no longer works? Also, the racist church has never embraced the laws to eliminate racism. I believe we are at the end. But there is hope yet. Reconciliation brings about a new beginning, the creation of the beloved community.

It is this type of spirit and this type of love that can transform oppressors into friends.

Therefore, if you bring your gifts to the altar, and there remember that if another has something against you, leave your gift there before the altar, and go your way. First, be reconciled to your brother, and then come and offer your gift. (Matthew 5:23-24)

Just as the African Americans initiated the Civil Rights Movement with a new sense of dignity and destiny despite injustice, exploitation, and the tragedy of slavery (physical/mental) they must now initiate reconciliation with justice during the racial divide in America. The initiation of reconciliation with justice must be outcome-driven.

The Greek language has three words for love: Eros, Philia, and Agape. Eros is a type of esthetic love. It has come to mean a sort of romantic love.

Philia is a sort of intimate affectionate between personal friends. This kind of love expects reciprocal love. Therefore, a person loves because he is loved, contrasted with when he is not loved.

The Greek language has a third word for love which is the highest level of love, agape. Agape means understanding, redeeming goodwill for all people. "Greater love has no one than this than to lay down one's life for his friends." (John 15:13) "Also you shall love your neighbor as yourself." (Leviticus 19:18) Further, you shall love your neighbor as yourself (Matthew 22:39). Finally, if you fulfill the royal law according to the scripture, "You shall love your neighbor as yourself, you do well; but if you show partiality, you commit sin, and are convicted by the law as transgressors." (James 2:8-9)

King used the love of God furnished by Christ's Spirit and motivation, while Gandhi provided the method to fight against collective evil in America's racism from 1956 to 1968.

Where do we go from here, America? King used to love as power during the period 1956-1968 and the Gandhi model to achieve justice, so we should use reconciliation through the spirit of Christ and the South African model of reconciliation with justice to achieve justice in this pivotal time of the century. We must, like our brothers and sisters in South Africa, who experienced Apartheid and similar inhumane treatment, rise to the beat of a different drum. We must embrace reconciliation. For reconciliation to truly take root, the oppressed must initiate the process rather than the oppressor. African Americans must accept reconciliation with justice as a process to remedy racism, forgive their oppressors, and press the oppressors to take ownership and negotiate reparations.

From 1954 to 1965, the Civil Rights Movement scored significant victories, while the United States gradually increased its military presence in the raging civil war in Vietnam. The noted scholar might around the globe was often against people of color. His point was validated in Hiroshima, Nagasaki, Korea, Vietnam, Iraq, and Afghanistan.

King maintained that the more tragic recognition of reality took place when it became clear that the war was doing far more than devastating the hopes of the poor at home. It was sending their male and female family members to fight and to die in extraordinarily high proportion compared to the rest of the population. African American young people who had been crippled by racism were being sent eight thousand miles away to guarantee liberties in Southeast Asia which they had not found in Southwest Georgia and East Harlem.

Also, King witnessed the reality that America had no real concern for its poor. The same reality exists today throughout urban America. The Personal Responsibility and Work Opportunity Reconciliation Act of 1996—Public Law 104-193 (PRWORA) ended aid to families with dependent children. The new federal programs imposed a maximum time limit of five years for a family to receive cash assistance and allow a state to set shorter time limits. Thousands of families and children have been forced deeper into poverty and homelessness. Somehow this madness must cease.

The words of the late John F. Kennedy (1961) will come back to haunt us. "Those who make peaceful revolution impossible will make violent revolution inevitable[14]." Increasingly, by choice or by accident, this is the role our nation has taken—the role of those who make peaceful revolution impossible by refusing to give up the privileges and the pleasures that come from the sinful, inhuman practice of systemic racism.

I am convinced that if we are to get on the side of the global world revolution, we as a nation must undergo a radical revolution of racial, multi-ethnic, multi-cultural values. We must rapidly begin the shift from a racist, white-oriented society to a person-oriented society (multi-ethnic). When machines and computers, profit motives, property rights, and western arrogance are considered more important than people, the giant triplets of racism, sexism, and poverty are incapable of being conquered.

A true revolution of racial, multi-ethnic, multi-cultural values will soon cause us to question the fairness and justice of many of our past and present policies.

People are important. All over the globe men and women are revolting against old systems of exploitation and oppression, and out of the wombs of a frail world new systems of justice and equality are being born. The shirtless and dehumanizing systemic institution of Apartheid has fallen, and the courage, wisdom, and love of the oppressed victims of Apartheid are practicing reconciliation.

Victims of oppression are sitting down with the oppressors seeking ways to remedy past injustices and forge ahead with equal justice for all. America must support these revolutions. However,

---

14

America must first be mature enough to look at its historic past and take ownership of its evil (collective evil in the institution of slavery), with its detrimental ongoing havoc heaped upon African Americans. Our hope today lies in our ability to recapture the revolutionary spirit and go out into sometimes hostile environments declaring hostility toward racism and poverty. With this powerful commitment, we shall boldly challenge the status quo and unjust racist society.

Awareness of this reality of escalating worldwide social, cultural, economic, and political interdependence and it's ironic and perplexing reassertion of particularism, crystallized under the banner of globalization during the early 1980s. A global perspective can help people recognize the need to explore diverse methods suitable for diverse contexts.

Scripture looks different in different settings; therefore, I am obligated to show how to actualize scripture in a North American context. A global perspective can help all people recognize the wonderful vitality and richness of the movement that begun when the "Word became flesh and lived among us." (John 1:14)

This call for a worldwide fellowship that lifts neighborly concern beyond one's race, class, gender, and nation is a call for an all-embracing and unconditional love for all people. This often misunderstood ad misinterpreted concept so readily discussed by the Nietzsche's of the world as a weak and cowardly force has now become an absolute necessity for the survival of humanity. I am speaking of that force that all the great religions have seen as the supreme unifying principle of life. Love is somehow the key that unlocks the door that leads to ultimate reality. This Hindu, Moslem Christian, Jewish, Buddhist belief about ultimate reality is found in scripture.

Let us love one another; for love is of God, and everyone that lived is born of God and knoweth God. He that loveth not knoweth not God, for God's love. If we love one another God dwelled in us; and his love is perfected in us. (1 John 3:11; 4:7-19)

Reconciliation with justice now! Let us begin. Now let us rededicate ourselves to the long and bitter but beautiful struggle for a new, inclusive community in the church and multi-cultural society in

America. The choice is ours, and though we might prefer it otherwise we must choose in this crucial moment of history.

King states that racism is a tenacious evil, but it is not insurmountable.

There must be a climate of social pressure in the African American community that scorns the Christian who does not pick up his citizenship rights and add his strength enthusiastically and voluntarily to the accumulation of power for himself and his people.

The past years have blown fresh winds of racism through urban America (the furor over the O.J. Simpson trial for example), but we are on the threshold of a significant change that demands a hundredfold acceleration. By 2021 ten of our larger cities will have a multi-ethnic (African American, Latino, Asians) majority population if present trends continue.

Camden, New Jersey, has elected its first Latino mayor (May 1997). We can shrug off this opportunity or use it for a new vitality to deepen and enrich our family and community life.

We must utilize the community-action groups and churches now proliferating in some urban slum areas to create not merely cultural identity, but a conscious, alert, and informed people who know their direction and whose collective wisdom and vitality commands respect. The result will be that the slave heritage can be cast into the dim past of our action; consciousness of our strength through reconciliation with justice and a resolute determination to use them in our daily experiences will evolve.

Justice is not the white man's birthright; it will be legislated for us and delivered in a neat government package. It is a social force any group can utilize by negotiating its elements in a principled, planned, deliberate strategy to achieve justice under its control.

The ongoing practice to ignore the African Americans' contribution to America's life and to strip them of their personhood is as old as the earliest history books and as contemporary as the morning's newspaper. To upset this cultural homicide, the African American must rise with an affirmation of Olympian human stature. In her widely read poem, "Still I Rise," Maya Angelou gives both a promise and a challenge: "but still like dust, I'll rise."

Any movement for African Americans' freedom that overlooks this necessity is only waiting to be buried. If the mind is enslaved, the body can never be free, Psychological freedom, a firm sense of self-esteem, is the most powerful weapon against the long night of physical slavery. No Lincoln's Emancipation Proclamation, Johnson's Civil Rights bill, nor Clinton's restatement of the affirmative action bill can bring this kind of freedom.

I believe the African-Americans will be free only when they reach down to the inner depths of their being and confront the oppressor on every level in this nation (the church, local government, institution, national government) at the bargaining table and say, "I forgive you for your wicked enslavement, racist superiority, white privilege, lynching, segregation, Jim Crow, separate-and-unequal education. Let's put that behind u. Now let's go forward with principled negotiated justice in America, for we, as a people, will never allow this church and government to enslave us again.

Let reconciliation with justice begin.

We, as a people, must throw off the manacles of self-abnegation and say to ourselves (and to the world)," I am free, with a rich and noble history. No matter how painful and exploited that history has been, I will never be a slave again. I will die, yes: I will fight and give my life before I will be a slave again."

America, this is my home, America this is my land, and America I own you. America you owe me. Together we are great, divided we will perish.

Up, you mighty race; you can accomplish what you will!

African Americans must continue the struggle, not for us alone, but all of America.

We have the God-given duty to help save ourselves and our white brothers and sisters from tragic self-destruction in the quagmire of racial hate.

This is a great hour for African Americans. The challenge is here. To become the instrument of a great idea is a privilege that history gives only occasionally.

This nation needs a transformation. African Americans could provide this transforming impulse only if they remain obedient to the

Spirit and teachings of Jesus Christ. African Americans must Forgive America for Slavery and all the implications resulting from Slavery.

Should the Southern Baptist church's resolution produce substantive changes, I believe they can join with black churches in this massive race war in the United States, will no longer be a novel if African American does not take the initiative in reconciliation with justice. (Matthew 5:23). I am convinced that African Americans cannot do it through hatred, they cannot do it through violence, they cannot do it by making the doctrine of black supremacy into a substitute for white supremacy. But they can do it by committing themselves to an active program of reconciliation with justice tempered with principled negotiation, a powerful positive love, and a deep understanding with love for all mankind (the Latinos, Asians, Jews, Moslems) and become one.

CHAPTER X

America needs Reconciliation, Forgiveness, and Healing

Biblical and Theological Basis of Reconciliation

In this chapter, we will explore the biblical and theological basis of reconciliation and its challenge to the church and America. A biblical mandate calls Christians and Evangelicals to a ministry of reconciliation. I Corinthians 5:19) Jesus is proclaimed Prince of Peace, and a special blessing is invoked for peacemakers identified as the children of God.

What are the processes necessary for our Nation to Becoming One?

There are potent examples of nations that have found a path moving forward on their way to Becoming One of reconciling…Germany and Israel; Canada and the Iroquois Nation; South African citizens. Yet, before any group embarks upon a path of healing, the wounds of the past must be confronted, confirmed, and condemned in a mutually beneficial manner.

This is not an easy proposition, but, as Bobby Kennedy reminds us, the rarest of commodities, Moral Courage, is also the most valuable and lasting. Our faith is largely based on forgiveness, and this one element is the cornerstone upon, which any reconciliation is constructed.

Nelson Mandela, Bishop Des Mond Tutu and the people of South Africa chose Reconciliation as oppose to Nuremberg Trials (1946).

Other elements of reconciliation that I describe in my book include repentance and justice, both of which lead to the final healing step, which is forgiveness.

I would also suggest that the backdrop for all to occur is a willingness to dialogue. Many of us pray each day for "Your Will Be Done." The virtues of peace and love and faith implore us to find the path of reconciliation, which includes the sacrifices, humility, and honor that comes with it along the way.

Yes…this is hard work. Yes…this uncomfortable. Yes… it may open old wounds. However, without the honest assessment of our past, reconciliation cannot be possible. And if reconciliation is not possible, then we find ourselves once again faking our place in the polarized side of our respective point of view.

And if we have no reconciliation, then the true and lasting potential of our nation will never be realized.

African Americans must forgive: Slavery, the Midnight Ride of the KKK, Jim Crow, Share Cropping, The Confederate/Statues and Monuments
White America must Repent and Compensate
Dialogue must become the tool for investigating and resolving Racial Discrimination complaints

CHAPTER XI

The Design of the Model

The case-study method was used to secure essential data about the churches participating in the consultation and to investigate racism and the principles for doing overcoming racism work. It was agreed that the method of getting information should be a guided interview to be done with the pastor, church leaders, and members. The interview questionnaire would be designed with questions to produce quantifiable data (yes/no, rating scales, and the likes) and qualitative data (examples) from open-ended questions. The consultant's role in helping to develop the interview questionnaire was not to decide what to ask, but how to ask, so that the questions would be as clear and as focused as possible. After several weeks of research, faxing, and meetings, one interview guide was developed for pastors, church leaders, and members, with most questions being the same on both forms. Before the first interview was conducted, a "training" workshop will be held to make sure that the interviewers are using the same style of "inviting" question asking, rather than leading the witness or putting words I'm the mouth of the witness.

The consultant's primary role is to enhance the integrity of the instruments used in gathering information and the integrity of the instruments used in gathering information and the integrity of the process in recording the information.

What Is the Case Method?

The use of the "case method" as distinguished from case histories commonly used in the medical field is preferable as a means of teaching and learning by the analysis of actual events. The approach originated in the Harvard Law School in 1870 and was later adopted by virtually all the law schools in the United States.

Rather than memorizing legal principles and theorizing about hypothetical situations, law students were thrust into the analysis of real cases as they were recorded. From the other student's analysis of the case, she/he was expected to make well-founded generalizations and to anticipate legal decisions based on sound rules of law.

In 1908 the Harvard Business School began to utilize cases from the business world as the central feature of its educational approach. The study of business dilemmas was formed to prepare the student for managerial positions by developing the skills needed for analyzing a situation and making tough decisions. Again, authentic events and situations where the data used in writing the cases. At times it was necessary to disguise the people or companies involved, but the facts were not altered in any way.

It was not until the 1960s that the first systematic attempts were made to employ the case method for the teaching of philosophy and theology, and then it was only by a very limited number of professors.

In 1971 the Association of Theological Schools (ATS) with the financial support of the Sealantic Fund began the Case Study Institute in Cambridge, Massachusetts. The Association for Case Teaching (ACT) was formed in 1977 by a group of graduates of the Case Study Institute. Through an annual national workshop for university and seminary faculty, focused seminars, and a variety of publications, ACT has attempted to provide educational resources to strengthen pedagogical skills and to make the teaching of social science theory more applicable to life experiences and more enjoyable. A case clearinghouse co-sponsored by ACT and Yale Divinity School Library includes nearly eight hundred cases written since 1971. Whereas the original Harvard law and business cases intentionally omitted references to personal relationships, most case studies written and published under the auspices of the Case Study Institute highlight the dimension of human relationships as an integral component of the dilemmas presented.

In the 1990s mediation and negotiation trainers in South Africa participating in the Empowering for Justice with Reconciliation Project adapted the case approach to their training in community conflict resolution. Rather than using cases written from a North American or wider African context, the trainers began writing cases that came directly from South African communities. They found that the process of objective analysis and group discussion of alternatives, particularly in racially and economically heterogeneous groups, honed skills of listening and broadening cultural understanding. Subsequent application of negotiation and mediation steps intensified and deepened participants' learning through role-play and scenarios drawn from the case study. The South African model in teaching conflict resolution is still being written.

What Is a Case?

A case is a carefully written description of an actual situation or event. All the data that one needs to enter vicariously into the problems are provided.

Most case situations, following the Harvard model, are seen through the eyes of one person who must make a critical decision.

Suggestions for How to Study a Case

A successful case discussion depends on careful preparation and on the interchange between participants to share insights and points of view. The following notes are some elementary hints on how to study a case. The following steps should enhance one's study:

Step 1. Immerse yourself in the case; get to know all the details. If possible, read the case several times. The racial and cultural context division must be considered.

Step 2. Analyze the case after reading it.
> Write out the cast of characters.
> Develop a chronology of events in the case.
> Identify the basic issues (especially those things, such as acts, values, and attitudes about which decision needs to be made).
> Try to see all the positions reasonable persons might take.

Step 3. Mull over the case, (i.e., think about it casually). Let things flow through your mind.

Step 4. Think of any theoretical material, which would help clarify or resolve the issues in the case.

Step 5. Remember that there is usually no one right answer.

Step 6. Participation
> Push your ideas; be willing to give reasons.
> Listen to others, evaluate their positions.
> Keep an open mind, be willing to change it upon new insights or evidence.
> Enjoy yourself.

Step 7. Remember the biblical mandate calls Christian to a ministry of reconciliation. (2 Corinthians 5:19). Jesus is proclaimed Prince of Peace, and a special blessing is invoked for peacemakers identified as the children of God. (Matthew 5:9)

The methodology for data analysis is to enter the quantifiable data into an SPSS (Statistical Program for the Social Science) computer file, report the frequency responses, and do a crosstab analysis of the data. An analysis of the recorded texts of the interviews would be done with a ranking of the number of times that those interviewed express the same thoughts.

The scheduling of interviews usually required two and three telephone calls.

Once scheduled, most of the interviewers are usually very professional and diligent in keeping their appointments.

However, there may be some very disappointing responses once the appointments are scheduled. This will be the most difficult, time-consuming, and costly process of the Cultural Audit. Nevertheless, the rewards are immense becoming one.

The Cultural Audit provides some key learning about the church, pastors, church leaders, and members. It is one too to be used in the development of goals, strategies, and priorities for embracing reconciliation with justice and overcoming racism.

A clear mandate for the church is to be at the forefront in helping people to value the diversity in their midst. There is a difference in inclusion and assimilation, and the church is challenged to become a truly inclusive community. The issue of diversity needs to be responded to in a variety of ways.

Important is the visible acceptance of diversity and the policy to include persons of different racial/ethnic groups, males and females. The church is called on to develop new models. A biblical basis for our stance on diversity is in place.

Congregation-based community organizing is a deliberate process of bringing religious congregations together around shared concerns and values to overcome racism and challenge social systems within the church to act justly. The organizing process includes:

Establishing relations between persons (who have overcome racism and clergy/leaders

Overcomers conducting a series of one-on-one or small community meetings to surface racism and build internal networks of relationships

Voting to select 1-2 racial problems on which the congregation will focus

Researching racial problems and determining long-term solutions for overcoming

Mobilizing networks for large public meetings to challenge appropriate officials around common issues and winning issues and repeating the process with even greater power and skill.

The congregational-based organization will:

Seek justice by calling for long-term, systemic ways to overcoming racism.

Break down ethnic and cultural barriers by bringing together people from diverse ethnic, religious, and racial backgrounds.

Encourage dialogue and action among religious congregations to do justice.

For example, seek congregations to voluntarily submit to the jurisdiction of the Pennsylvania Human Relations Commissions' mandates.

Meet and discuss racial issues with public officials face to face in a large public setting.

Rely on broad-based, collective leadership among many people.

Develop leaders to speak and act on behalf of overcoming racism and becoming one.

Principles for Doing, Overcoming Racism Work

Accountable, Monitoring and Self-Determination
For us to be successful on our journey toward overcoming racism, we must acknowledge a relationship of accountability to each other in several significant ways.
For all of us, European Americans, African-Americans, Asian Americans, and Hispanic Americans, we need the support and nurturing that this kind of relationship will provide, since nothing I'm our world/culture/society (outside of this relationship) encourages us to

do that which is necessary to overcome racism. Rather, everything that we know to be the truth informs that things must remain "as they are."

Accountability requires mutuality. White people must establish a community in which they are accountable to each other in overcoming racism. People of color must be accountable to other people of color in this community who are dedicated to dismantling internalized oppression. Further, James Cone, (God of the Oppressed) says that white people must be like babies when they join the liberation struggle. Just as babies need guidance and direction so too, do white people when they attempt to address racism. People of color are the experts of the effects, impact/pain/suffering/death that racism has on them. White people are the agents responsible for the harsh, cruel, inhuman results. Therefore, those people of color in the community working on overcoming racism must provide direction, guidance, and monitoring to white people engaged in this struggle. Most importantly, we must all be accountable to the larger community of which we are a part and which we serve.

In our working community, white people must constantly self-monitor whose norms and standards are being used when structuring the group when making decisions, and when using language. People of color in the working community must monitor white people when they are doing their overcoming-racism work.

Monitoring is a relationship based on sharing, the sharing of experiences, information, care and feelings, and mutual respect. It is observed that harm may be done by white people in their activity.

People of color will consult with one another and arise at a collective response designed to alleviate the situation.

In this way, the community will be protected from harm done through ignorance or misunderstanding of how racism impacts people of color.

People of color have the additional responsibility of doing work on themselves.

Determination, self-determination, is the ability or right to name oneself, speak for oneself, and defend oneself.

This work will enable people of color to understand more freely their predicament, to discern what action or decisions will be in their best interests, and to provide informed, appropriate leadership to white people engaged in overcoming racism activity.

Self-determination must include creating the climate for white people to dialogue about their beliefs, attitudes, assumptions, theories, and their practice of racism, Self-determination is denied unless white people "choose" who will be the monitor. Racism does not go away because we are not looking; nor will it go away when we ignore it, as in just don't pay attention. People of color continue to be hurt.

Accountability is a process that requires education, reflection, and action.

Education may be done on an individual basis or as a group activity. From education comes the need to reflect on what has been learned by a discussion with others who have shared the learning experience and by discerning our reflective learning in the mirror, which is the larger community to whom we are accountable. In this way, we continue to monitor ourselves and our group to present working in a vacuum with only one group's norm and standards prevailing, Education and Reflection Lead to Action.

When taking any action, we maintain our accountability to our community by listening, checking things out, and taking appropriate action based on continued communication. Action leads back to more education, reflection, and action, thus becomes an ongoing, life-long process of change.

Internalized Oppression

What is "internalized oppression?" This is a phenomenon peculiar to people who have been kidnapped or held hostage for a protracted period. The captive begins to identify with or even defend their captors (the Patty Hearst Syndrome). However, there is a form of internalized oppression that is far more widespread, affecting many more people but is very seldom discussed, defined, or even acknowledged. It is the demon (or the elephant in the living room that no one talks about) that affects African Americans and other people of color who have endured, suffered, and survived the oppression of racism.

One of the great tragic consequences of racism is that, at some point, I will be forced to talk about racism and what it means. I will need to clarify my position on racism when I truly only want to discuss internalized oppression, because "internalized oppression" and racism have conspired to confuse us about just who is a "racist" in this society.

Racism is the way of life constructed by and for white people. It is the institutionalization of the racial prejudice of white people: white people invented the concept of "race," establishing "white" as the norm for humanity, the standard by which all others are measured. Once white people defined themselves as epitomizing the best, most desirable qualities of human beings, it naturally follows that others (people of color) are defined as less than that, with black people having the least desirable qualities of humanity. This belief in the supremacy of "whiteness" resulted in the racist way of life, which is to say that all people other than white people became excluded from every endeavor considered to be among the rights or purview of human beings, legal, social, political, and cultural. White people reserved "power" for them, "power" being the legitimate access to system sanctioned by the state. Racism is race prejudice combined with the power to enforce that prejudice.

But there remains within the small community of folks who are struggling with understanding and dismantling internalized oppression, some basic disagreement not only with how to describe the situation but also with exactly what to call it. Terms such as internalized racism," "internalized racist oppression," "Uncle Thomism" all have been used to describe this largely unrecognized social phenomenon.

Simply put, internalized oppression is the survival response of people of color to the oppression of racism. It is the way of life that enables us to suffer through and endure, and yes, even overcomes the deadly machinations of racism that plague our lives. (Dr. A. Roger Reddick is an overcomer of racism.)

Internalized oppression is characterized by participation in stereotyped behavior, self-hate, low self-esteem, assimilation of alien values, negative self-image, and defender of the status quo.

When we begin to evaluate ourselves considering the "program" we have or have not made, we need to look at what we have lost as a result of our oppression under white supremacy. First, and perhaps most significantly, we have lost (rather, it has been stolen from us) the right of self-determination. We can no longer define or describe who we are as human beings, where we came from, or even what we are named, both as individuals and as people bound by common culture and history. That human entitlement, described in the American Declaration of Independence as the "right to life, liberty, and the pursuit of happiness," has been abrogated for us by those who have determined to what extent and under what condition people of color may pursue life, liberty, and happiness.

We have been told and we have accepted ("internalized") as fact, that we are not a people of greatness, achievement, and value to human society. We have accepted the notion that the way we look, talk, act, and feel is an anathema to the world, and so we diligently seek approval by modifying those attributes to conform to the prevailing standards set by others.

Working on internalized oppression involves a close examination of how we relate to each other as individuals, to our children, to other members of our community, and our response to leadership and acceptance of internalized stereotypes.

We must begin to discuss the pattern of behavior that reveals the hatred from ourselves imposed on us by racism: rage, fear, indignation, frustration, powerlessness, criticism, fault-finding, and destruction of self-confidence. We must begin to re-create an image of self on our behalf: then and only then will we be able to discern what we need to do for ourselves and what help if any we need from others.

Internalized oppression tells us that we must wait and work hard for the acceptance and approval of white people. Internalized oppression informs us of the correctness of the language of equality versus inequality or superiority versus inferiority. If we accept the language that describes our Civil Rights Movement as a "struggle for equality," and then we accept the inference that we are, in fact, not equal to those who have spent much time and effort toward having us believe that we are "three-fifths of a man." When we do the work of overcoming racism, it will become apparent that acceptance and approval must be on God's terms, for we stand as equals in the community of humankind.

African Americans:

It must create a climate for the majority population to discuss and be told about the meaning of racism.

African Americans must stop separating at the table; they must impact the table (black Professor at Princeton, black students at Harvard, black legislators in congress, black United Methodist Pastors.

Must build relationships with other ethnic groups, and severe the Jewish economic strangulation (Hispanics and African Americans should call a summit and discuss a third party)

Support African American institutions with big bucks and build new ones.

Initiate the dialogue to overcome racism on God's terms and God's conditions.

Patterns of Internalized Oppression

Any experienced hurt or mistreatment that has not been discharged will create distress patterns. As a result, this distressing pattern is re-stimulated. It forces the victimized person to reenact the original distress experience with others (usually someone less threatening).

The inability to discharge this hurt/mistreatment instills chronic distress patterns within the victimized person. He/she is not to blame for the initiation and installation of these patterns.

The necessary conditions do not exist for the oppressed person to reenact these patterns upon the oppressors (discharge).

This circumstance becomes a self-fulfilling prophecy whereby the victimized person further victimizes her/himself and others.

Operational patterns, in individual relations' dramatization of feelings of fear, rage indignation, frustration, and powerlessness are directed at each other.

Then comes the invalidation of our children with harsh criticism and faultfinding intending to "straighten them out" but instead destroying self-confidence. Then there is a group effort of finding fault, criticizing, and invalidating each other as adults.

Terms and Definitions Necessary for Doing, Overcoming Racism Work

Racism:
a rejection of the teachings of Jesus Christ. We commit ourselves as individuals and as a community to follow Jesus Christ in word and deed and unite our efforts to overcome all forms of institutional racism.

Prejudice:
an adverse judgment or opinion formed beforehand or without knowledge or examination; the act or state of holding unreasonable preconceived judgments or convictions.

Discrimination:
an action based on prejudice.

Stereotype:
a conventional and/or over-simplified conception, opinion, or belief, based on prejudice and often negative.

Bigotry:
intolerance. An action based on a stereotype. There is no power relationship necessarily implied or expressed by "prejudice," discrimination, stereotype or bigotry."

Race:
an arbitrary socio-political category created by Europeans in the 15th century used to assign human worth and social status to themselves as the model of humanity, to establish white-skin access to sources of power.

White:
when referring to people, this term was created by Virginian slave owners and colonial rulers in the 17th century.

It replaced terms like "Christian" and "Englishman" (sic) to distinguished European colonists from each other and Africans and indigenous peoples. European indentured servants of European and of African descent ha united against the colonial elite. The legal creation of "white" meant giving privileges to some while denying them to others with the justification of biological and social inferiority. Thus "white" is a political, not a cultural term. As a result, "white" became a political construct, the effect of which is systemic Apartheid. On this construct, the way of life known as racism effectively was built.

White Privilege: white privilege is a right, favor, advantage, immunity, specially granted to white individuals or groups, and withheld from others. White privilege is an unearned asset about which white people are usually oblivious. "White people were exempt from slavery, land grab, and genocide, the first forms of white privilege (in the future U.S.)." U.S. institutions and culture give preferential treatment to peoples whose ancestors came from Europe over people whose ancestors came from the Americas, Africa, Asia, and the Middle East; and exempt European-Americans (white peoples) from the forms of racial and national oppression inflicted upon peoples from the Americas, Africa, Asia, and the Middle East. The web of preferential treatment and exemption is called white privilege.

White Supremacy: a historically based, institutionally perpetuated system of exploitation and oppression of people of color, nations, and continents by white peoples and nations of the European continent to maintain and defend a system of wealth, power, and privilege.

Power:

The ability or capacity to act; strength of force extended or capable of being exerted; might; the ability or official capacity to exercise control. "Power" is a relational term. It can be understood as the relationship between human beings in a specific historical, economic, and social setting. It must be exercised to be visible. Exploitative power" is the most destructive. It identified power with force. Its subject's persons to whatever use they may have to the person/group who holds the power. Manipulative power is power over another. Competitive power is power against another and promotes rivalry and destructive personal influence. Nutrient power is power for the other, given by one's care for others coming out of concern for the welfare of the group. Integrative power is power with others, involving responsibility and accountability.

Power is the ability to define reality and has other people respond to your definition as if it were their own.

Racism:

Racism is race prejudice plus the exploitative and manipulative power to enforce that prejudice. Racism is a system of oppression based on race that in this country is perpetrated by white people against people of color. It involves an unequal distribution of systemic power for people with white skin privilege in four main areas: 1) the power to make and enforce decision; 2) the power to control and/or limit access to resources, broadly defined; 3) the ability to set and determine standards for what is considered appropriate behavior, and 4) the ability to define reality. Racism also includes the power of white people to blame people of color for racism. Racism is manifested personally, culturally, and institutionally. It is a system that both upholds the power of white people and undermines the power of people of color. The responsibility of perpetuating and legitimizing a racist system rests both on those who actively maintain it, and on those who refuse to challenge it.

A Racist:

one who is both privileged and socialized based on race by the white supremacist (racist) system; one who uses, participates in, or benefits from racism as defined above. The term applies to all white people living in the United States, regardless of class, gender, religion, culture, or sexuality.

A Non-racist: This term was created by white people to deny responsibility for systemic racism, to maintain an aura of innocence in the face of racial oppression, and to shift responsibility for that oppression from white people to people of color (called "blaming the victim").

An Anti-racist: as applied to white people, an anti-racist is a person who grows in understanding the effects and toll of racism on her/himself, including her/his spiritual alienation. Such a person makes a conscious choice to act to challenge some aspect of the white supremacy system, including his/her white privilege. That person engages in deconstructing racism (see 11 below).

The transformation required to become an anti-racist is not an easy one to make for European-American/white folks.

European-American white folks need others for a long-term commitment. As applied to People of Color some use the term anti-racist.

Others use the term such as activist, freedom fighter, or liberation fighter. In practice, it is difficult for an activist of color not to be an anti-racist activist, since the struggle against racial oppression intersects with every issue affecting the people of color.

Classic Racist Behaviors: There are a least four classic racist behaviors. 1) The difficultly of white folk in listening to people of color: often is solely a cognitive level and marked by defensiveness and a readiness to deny and/or trivialize in such a way as not to hear or discern the message being conveyed by people of color. 2) The invalidation by white folk of the experience of people of color: often based on the refusal to acknowledge world views other than that of the white European-American. 3) The unwillingness of white folk to take direction from people of color: in the development of an anti-racist agenda; often marked by an unwillingness to restructure the norms and/or to share access to resources. 4) The usurpation of the personal and collective sovereignty of persons of color by white folks, often marked by attempts to manipulate the self-determination and agenda of people of color.

Anti-racist Behavior: behavior marked by listening, by valuing the experience of people of color, by a willingness to take direction and to be held accountable, and by support for the self-determination and the agenda of people of color.

Reverse Racism: a term created and used by white people to deny their white privilege. It refers to affirmative-action policies that allegedly give "preferential treatment" to white people and to describe the behavior of people of color when they act to oppression.

Reverse Discrimination and Affirmative Action: Racists are quick to blame white male unemployment on African Americans and affirmation action. They insist that there are fewer jobs because African Americans are getting all the work.

But black economic progress has not been at the expense of whites. Indeed, despite advances by blacks, whites remain in control of 99.7% of the nation's gross national product.... Affirmative action programs have had little effect on white employment. A recent study of state contracts in Louisiana found that although African Americans comprise a large percent of the state population, the state awards less than five percent of its contracts to minorities. If affirmative action compromised opportunities for white males, the bulk of the criticism would be directed toward white women, the greatest beneficiaries of affirmative action."

Oppressors, Oppressed, Oppression: an oppressor uses personal/group power to dominate others and refuses to use personal/group power to challenge forms of oppression. The oppressed (person or group) are dominated by an oppressor and by those who consent with their silence. Oppression is the powerful effect of domination.

Internalized Oppression: the situation that occurs in a racist system when a racial group oppressed by racism supports the supremacy and dominance of the dominating group by maintaining or participating in the set of attitudes, behaviors, social structures, and ideologies that undergird the dominating group's power. Internalized oppression results in the assimilation and reflection of values and social systems from the dominant group. "Many of these values tend to imitate and intensify the effects of racism[15]."

Deconstructing Racism: the work of an anti-racist (see the previous definition). There are two paths to the same goal: 1) The agenda of white folk is to understand racism, their participation in it, and the effects of racism on their humanity, to commit to self-education and collective education, and to undo and dismantle the system of racism. 2) The agenda of people of color is to understand racism and their own internalized oppression, to commit to self-education and collective education, and to undo and dismantle internalized oppression.

Accountability for Deconstructing Racism: White folks are accountable to each other. People of color are accountable to each other. White folk is accountable to people of color regarding their racism.

Biblical Foundation for Dealing with Racial Conflict

What is the conflict? It is derived from the Latin conflicts, meaning to strike together. Webster's Third International Dictionary defines conflict as a clash, competition, or mutual interference of opposing or incompatible forces or qualities (such as ideas, interests, or wills). Conflict occurs when there are differences between individuals or groups over resources, needs, or values. What is the biblical foundation for understanding and dealing with conflict? The following clusters of passages help to share a biblical perspective on conflict:

15

Christian Friendship Demands Mutual Correction:

James 5:16 95;13-15
Galatians 6:2 (6:1-5
2 Samuel 12:1-4
Matthew 23
The Controversy Between Peter and Paul
Act 5:1-11
Galatians 2:11-13 (2:11-21)
2 Peter 3:14-18
The Christian Is to Resist "the World"
1 Corinthians 2:12-14 Ephesians 2:1-2
Romans 2:21 2 Corinthians 1:18-25
Mark 4:18-19 John 17:6-8, 15-19
Suffering Servant / Crucifixion Passages
Isaiah 42:1-4
Isaiah 53:1-7 (53:1-12)
Luke 43:44-46
Non-Violent Resistance
Matthew 5:38-48
Matthew 26:51-54
Act 5:27-32
Jesus' Life and Other Guidelines
2 Corinthians 5:14-21
John 17:6-8, 15-19, 20-26

The Urgency to Overcome Racism Is Echoed Throughout Former President Obama's Speech on Race

The urgency to overcome racism is echoed throughout President Obama's Speech on Race, given while he was candidate Obama. The evils of racism have been addressed on many levels and from many angles. However, the subject of the urgency in addressing racism is somewhat unique. Indeed, much of what is written on the broader subject can lead us to conclude that the pervasiveness of racism and its systemic nature renders any near-term solution unattainable. From this can come a complacency that will undermine a sense of urgency in the fight against this evil, Therefore, this topic is timely and important. Obama's Speech on Race was forced as a result of racism alarms from the candidates' foot soldiers' encounters with name-calling, vandalism, bomb threats, and meeting cruel reactions. The bigotry has gone beyond words. In Vincennes, the Obama Campaign Office was vandalized at 2 A.M. on the eve of the primary. A large plate-glass window was smashed; an American flag was stolen. Other windows were spray-painted with references to Obama's controversial former pastor, Rev. Jeremiah Wright, and other political messages: "Hamas votes BHO," and "We don't cling to guns or religion. Goddamn Wright" (MSNBC.com). I predict the worst of Racism will come when the honeymoon with Mr. Obama ends sometime around 2010 when the Emergency Economic Stimulus fails to reach the middle class and spearhead an upsurge in the economy. Unfortunately, Mr. Obama lacked the Moral Courage to set in motion any dialogue to Overcome Racism through dialogue. Therefore, we are seeking President Donald Trump to display his Moral Courage and set in motion dialogue as a tool to overcome Racism.

Root Causes of Racism

A misunderstanding of the root causes of racism can lead to the complacency we mentioned above. Such a misunderstanding can also lead us astray in our effort to combat racism and make our best-intentioned efforts ineffectual. Therefore, let us be clear about the basis for racism that we might understand just as clearly the way it must be overcome.

Obama's Race Speech was combining constructive dialogue, study, and action. It was examining the current state of race relations and our common future, looking at existing laws and policies, and recommending new ones that could help to ensure that we remain one America. Its enlisted individuals, communities, business, and government at all levels to understand our differences as we appreciate the values that unite us.

Why a major speech race? While running for President Obama saw for himself the great harm caused by racial discrimination and the difference that could be achieved by changing attitudes. That longstanding, deeply personal commitment led him to make this speech one of its major speeches in his campaign. He knew that America could reach its full potential only by enlisting the full energies of all our people and by giving all our citizens, of every background, the chance to make the most of their God-given talents.

That was not a crisis, but an opportunity. This effort built on the president's record throughout his campaign (defending affirmative action, delivering major speeches economics, foreign policy, hope, yes, we can, and now on race and reconciliation). But unlike previous speeches in this area, President Obama's Race Speech was the result not of a crisis, but a unique opportunity.

America is strong enough to look to the future. America moved aggressively in the present to elect the first African American president—reversing the past tide of rejection of Jessie Jackson, Shirley Chisholm, and others, and inequality. Candidate Obama believes that it was time for America to address the issue of race relations as we prepared for the 21st century.

Many "wedges" issues had been defused. On many of the issues that had been used to divide the country—such as race and religion—Candidate Obama had begun to change the terms of the debate, pointing to solutions instead of pointing fingers, and defusing tensions so that an honest dialogue about race could begin.

Responsibility, Community, and Citizenship

This speech would encourage us Americans to take responsibility for ourselves, our families, and our community. It was a call to citizenship because the future president believed that being a good citizen included recognizing the promise of America—America free of destructive bigotry, a nation that welcomes those who play by the rules, and a country of people that value and serve their communities.

The future president's Speech on Race is embodied in Becoming One. This book provides a tool for the implementation of the future president's speech and his commitment to One America, One Nation, and One People. This book could aid the president with strategies to achieve these goals.

Through dialogue, study and action, we could increase our understanding of race, and propose and promote policies and solutions that could make a difference.

Constructive Dialogue

Constructive dialogue can help to inform and to build support for constructive solutions to the issues of race. For an entire generation growing up after the Civil Rights Movement, there has been little or no public attention to the values and ideals of racial reconciliation. Unfortunately, the little rhetoric present in public discourse has too often been negative, helping to perpetuate derogatory stereotypes. This Initiative would employ the power of the presidency to encourage open, candid debate about difficult issues and to highlight actions by individuals, communities, businesses, and governments that were working in this area now.

Study

The issues to be addressed include exploring different perceptions and experiences of Americans of different races, confronting harmful stereotypes, and examining serious problems that stand in the way of racial reconciliation. While the initiative would be largely forward-looking, it would also be important to help educate Americans about the past so that the nation had a clear understanding of what has come before.

Action

Throughout this effort, attention would go to policies that could make a difference and solutions that could be implemented by individuals, community groups, businesses, state and local governments, and the federal government. This nation can make real progress in overcoming racism. Overcoming racism principles must be taught throughout communities in America. President Obama's grassroots community organizations could be the ISG for the implementation of the Becoming One model for overcoming racism. Nearly a quarter of America's colleges and universities and all the nation's Human-Relations Commissions could partner with the president's Initiative on Race to encourage every college and university to conduct special programs focusing on race and other dimensions of diversity in American society. Obama's Speech on Race should be the foundation of the nation's first Cabinet-level appointment for Overcoming Racism for all Americans. The One America: Conversations that bring us together time is now.

Summary Reflections/Understandings

Whatever European-Americans/white folks do deeply affect people of color.
People of color do not have the institutional power to resist institutionally what European-American/white folk are doing.
European-American/white folks can be responsible or irresponsible to people of color.
The choices European-American white people make create situations to manipulate the agendas of people of color.
The decisions of European-American/white people affect the ability of people of color to function.
European-American/white people—affects people of color by forcing them to confront or participate in behaviors or agendas that are not necessarily in their best self-interests.

Summary

Diversity has become a hot-button word that denotes a multitude of meanings and is a word that can easily be misconstrued. That is often the problem with words that have a broad meaning, but which are commandeered by narrowly focused interests. At our Becoming One Enrichment and Diversity Center, we believe it is important to differentiate between words... and intentions. Yes... we are committed to "diversity." It is the name of our charitable organization. But we deploy diversity as a working template to unify our nation and to unlock the enormous potential that inclusiveness has proven to foster in America.

The love and compassion that diversity creates, changes mind and heart. Aristotle says, "educating the mind without educating the heart is no education at all." This manuscript educates America on Racism, dialogue as a tool to Overcome Racism, and embrace Diversity because Diversity makes America Great.

America is a great country and has many marvelous things in it. We have one of the world's largest economies, very good job opportunities, and we invest money in important things such as our education and people. Below are a few things I think make America great.

The first is our education. We are number two in the world when it comes to education. Total expenditures for public elementary and secondary schools in the United States in 2015–16 amounted to $706 billion, or $13,847 per public school student enrolled in the fall. We even have the top five best colleges in the world. As part of a military family, I have moved a lot and have attended many different schools. In each of the schools I have been to, you can tell that the teachers, school board, and even the government care about the students and puts a lot of money and time into the education they offer.

The second is our diversity. We have a lot of diversity in this country, and that makes us who we are as a country. It also makes us unique from other countries. Diversity can also spark creativity, drive innovation, and can help people learn more about different cultures. Diversity can also help us view and understand different perspectives of the world in which we live. Diversity can increase our adaptability and can increase our innovation and collaboration.

Last, I want to bring up the most important thing that makes America great, the people. People in this country selflessly serve in the military. Every year, thousands of people enlist in and join the many different branches of the military. People also fill other important roles. If we didn't have teachers, we would not be educated. If we didn't have a president or leader, it would be chaotic. As I said in an earlier point, we have many people of different ethnicities that make up our country and make us unique. All my other points in this essay would not be possible without people. People play a vital role in shaping America into what it is today.

Education is a crucial part of America. Diversity can help us grow in knowledge. People are what make this country. All three of these are very important unique things that make America great.

The biracial population is exploding in America due to an increase in Mixed marriages (Black men and white women and white men and Black women). This is an example of a Biracial student experience at The University of North Carolina in Chapel Hill, North Carolina: I am biracial: my mother is Filipina-American, and my father is African American. Whenever I introduce myself to others, this is one of the first facts I reveal about myself to them. Although some people make it clear to me that bringing up race is exhausting and uncomfortable to them, to me it is necessary- my racial background plays such a huge role in my everyday experiences and interactions with others. My mixed ethnicity is a part of me that defines the blend of cultures and practices that shaped me into how I perceive the world: with open eyes.

Sometimes I feel that people form opinions about me based on what they prefer to see rather than who I truly am. People look at my physical characteristics- curly hair, full lips- and choose to see me as simply black. They then associate me with stereotypes of black culture, which are not always positive. Meanwhile, I have a mother that exposes me to her Filipino culture every day and spends time cooking traditional meals for my family. She has introduced me to music and television from the Philippines and helps me keep in regular contact with my cousins abroad. She shares her enthusiasm for her home country each day, yet people react to me as if I lack her influence in my life.

On the contrary, some individuals do not see me as black enough. They examine every aspect of my life to find reasons to revoke my metaphorical "black card". When I hear that I am not black enough for people's expectations, it is infuriating. Despite what people choose to believe about my race, I cannot forget the brutal incidents of racial injustice that my grandparents experienced and described to me. To disregard my blackness is to brush off the efforts my grandparents made toward me. I understand that people always form preconceived notions about others but invalidating someone's identity is ignorant and inconsiderate.

I can recall one time when I first realized how different I was. My family made a long trip to Jollibee- Filipino fast-food restaurant hours away. My parents and I reminisced on the days that we ate there during our trips to the Philippines, and my younger sister had never been before. I remember thinking about how amazing it was that I could visit a Jollibee in the United States. I thought I would feel a familiar, at-home feeling when we went, but the reality was different. Everyone there had straight hair like my mother and spoke the foreign Tagalog tongue. These elements were familiar to me, as throughout my entire life I was surrounded by Filipino culture through my mother and her friends. Yet as I stepped foot in the restaurant, all eyes were on my family. We were literally and metaphorically "the black sheep". As we walked in, heads turned up to examine and exchange looks from across meals. However, my family ordered our food, enjoyed it, and had an amazing time. That moment was a turning point in the awareness I had regarding my race. Rather than feeling set apart from the rest, I realized the importance of being certain in who I was instead of seeking validation from others. If I understand that I am equally black as I am Asian, then it should not matter how others view me. It should not concern me that both sides sometimes consider me as an outsider. I learned how significant it was that not everyone has the opportunity of being exposed to as many cultures and mindsets as I have. I appear racially ambiguous and I know that I can use it to change others' close-minded views of the world.

Although it can sometimes cause some difficulty, racial ambiguity has its benefits. It often forces me to take the role of the middleman or leader and unite people. I meet people who I may not have met had I not been biracial and introduce them to people that they typically would not become close to either. Being biracial allows me to see the differing views of others as well, even beyond race. Learning to embrace diversity has made me view the world with an open mind. Being biracial has also taught me to look at every side of a problem and its solutions. I have learned to value everyone's beliefs and to respect them whether I agree- even in cases in which others do not take them seriously (because I know what that feels like). Everyone deserves respect, and I am glad that my own experiences help me stand up for that belief.

What is alarming about this exploding population is that some do not want to be Black or White. Imagine the diversity at their dinner table and the negative racial encounters they experience every day. Therefore, we must overcome Racism and dialogue is the best tool to initiate that process addressed in.

Are we so intent on "being right" that it clouds our ability to "do what's right?" Is our emphasis on what's right for me or what's right for our community?

It is our choice to do what's right for the greater good. No false dichotomy here.

With that, our challenge now is to spread the good news about how service and selflessness are not only good for uniting our country/ community but are some of the most fulfilling work any of us can do working to Become coming to one America.

President Donald J. Trump signed into law what proponents say is the most comprehensive federal prison reform bill in decades. Trump signed the bipartisan evangelical-backed First Step Act at the oval office of the White House joined by criminal justice reform advocates, faith leaders, ex-offenders, and lawmakers who've pushed hard to pass the bill.

2019 Prison Reform Act is aimed at reducing recidivism and refining sentencing laws and harsh penalties. The Prison Reform Bill also aims to help ex-convicts rebuild their lives after their release from prison.

The U.S. Senate approved the Act with a vote of 87 to 12, and the house signed it 358-36. Thank you, Mr. President, Donald Trump, for your moral courage and we believe that you can help America establish dialogue as a tool to overcome racism.

Notes

1. Albert Reddick, Becoming One the USA and Diversity. Publish América, LLLP, 2009

2. Dietrich Bonhoeffer. The Cost of Discipleship. (New York: MacMillan Company, 1963) p.89

3. Dietrich Bonhoeffer, The Communion of Saints, Act and Being, Christ the Center, Creation, and Fall. (1933)

4. John Kennedy (1961)

5. Hannah Arendt (1984) 18

6. Gregory L. Jones, Embodying Forgiveness: A Theological Analysis. (Grand Rapids, MI.: William B. Eerdmans Publishing Company, 1994).

7. Ibid.

8. W.E.B. Dubois, The History of the American Negro (1903).

9. Scott M. Peck, The Different Drum: Community Making and Peace, (Simon & Schuster, 1987).

10. Ron Sider. One-Sided Christianity: Uniting the Church to Heal a Lost and Broken World.

11. Grand Rapids, MI.: Zondervan Publishing House, 1993).

12. Peter Paris, Overcoming Alienation in Theological Education, Shifting Boundaries:

13. Contextual Approaches to the Structures of Theological Education.

14. Ron Sider, One-Sided Christianity, 36.

www.ingramcontent.com/pod-product-compliance
Lightning Source LLC
LaVergne TN
LVHW041851070526
838199LV00045BB/1548